GOD

IS DISAPPOINTED
IN YOU

written by
MARK RUSSELL

cartoons by
SHANNON WHEELER

Top Shelf Productions

Mark would like to thank Kalah Allen, Sarah Arndt,
his support group at Writers Anonymous, and Nora Robertson,
without whom this book would have never happened.

Shannon would like to thank his lucky stars for not getting
hit by lightning (as did his mom). Also, thanks to Patricia
(who survived a lightning hit), Richard, Rani, Austin,
Berkeley, Max, and Thelonious. And finally a thanks to
Mark for letting me be a part of this awesome project.
I hope it doesn't get us killed.

God Is Disappointed In You © 2013 Mark Russell and Shannon Wheeler.

Published by Top Shelf Productions, an imprint of IDW Publishing, a division of Idea
and Design Works, LLC. Offices: Top Shelf Productions, c/o Idea & Design Works, LLC,
2765 Truxtun Road, San Diego, CA 92106. Top Shelf Productions®, the Top Shelf logo,
Idea and Design Works®, and the IDW logo are registered trademarks of Idea and Design
Works, LLC. All Rights Reserved. With the exception of small excerpts of artwork used
for review purposes, none of the contents of this publication may be reprinted without
the permission of IDW Publishing. IDW Publishing does not read or accept unsolicited
submissions of ideas, stories, or artwork.

Editor-in-Chief: Chris Staros.
Edited by Chris Staros and Leigh Walton.
Designed by Chris Ross.

Visit our online catalog at www.topshelfcomix.com.

Sixth Printing, February 2021. Printed in China.

ISBN 978-1-60309-098-8

CONTENTS

THE NEW TESTAMENT 139

PREFACE

HE **BIBLE MAY BE THE SINGLE MOST IMPORTANT BOOK IN** human history. It has inspired no fewer than three of the world's major religions. Four, if you count Mormons. People look to the Bible for guidance on everything from bombing another country to entering the cheese competition at the County Fair. But it's my guess that of the more than a billion people who claim to live according to the teachings of the Bible, not too many of them know what the Bible actually says. They, like me prior to writing this book, probably only know the tiny morsel of the Bible that was spoon-fed to them in Sunday School. The rest of the Bible remains a sort of religious hot dog, something they eat on faith without having the first clue of what's actually in it.

When I began this project, I quickly became astonished to realize just how little I knew about the Bible, despite growing up in church and attending Christian schools, where I was taught the Bible as a daily routine. How many stories my teachers had sanitized, omitted, or just gotten wrong. How many dark, hilarious, or truly profound passages the Bible contained that I was never taught, probably because all anyone really wanted me to learn was how to sit quietly, eat my carrots, and feel guilty.

Whatever the case, no one ever really taught me what the Bible was, or why I should love it. This is an oversight I hope to correct with this book. I give you the entire Bible, albeit condensed down to its very essence. I also tried to incorporate a little historical background to give what you're about to read some much-needed context. It was my aim to take each of the sixty-six books of the Bible on its own terms, including the stories you were probably never meant to hear, and yet, eliminating all the interminable genealogies, arcane language and repetition that has probably kept you from reading the Bible yourself.

When reading this book, the first question to cross your mind will probably be, "Is this really in the Bible?" The short answer is yes. The dialogue and phrasing is mine, of course. For example, none of the books of the Bible were written in a Q&A format. Presenting Habakkuk and Hebrews this way was a stylistic choice on my part.

Also, James never called anyone a "prick," as far as I know. And the astute observer might note that King David never actually went through a heavy metal phase, though some of his lyrics could have easily found a home in Dio-era Sabbath. Certainly I use my own language and allegories to make the work translate to a modern audience, though my intention is always to describe the events and their meanings just as they were written in the Bible thousands of years ago.

I am joined in this work by Shannon Wheeler, award-winning cartoonist for the *New Yorker* and the creator of *Too Much Coffee Man*. It was hard enough for me to squeeze each book of the Bible down to two or three pages each. Shannon had the unenviable task of boiling them down into a single panel, and in doing so, making it even easier to absorb. This is by no means a new strategy. In fact, this is the basic concept behind cathedrals. When people were bored by the bishop's sermon, they could always look around at the stained-glass windows and enjoy the glowing cartoons of Jonah getting swallowed by a whale, or John the Baptist getting his head lopped off. When you're trying to explain something complicated, visual aids never hurt.

It is not my intention to mock the Bible with this book, nor to endorse it, but merely to present it on its own terms in a way that is accessible and which relays the same sense of fascination I had when I truly discovered the Bible for the first time. If you want to reject the Bible as ancient superstition or follow it as the holy word of God, that's up to you. I just thought you might like to know what's actually in the hot dog.

—Mark Russell

THE OLD TESTAMENT

"Can't you do that someplace else?"

PART ONE
THE TORAH

In which God gets the human race on the road and then threatens to stop the car, the Jews receive 613 easy-to-follow rules, and a haircut topples a nation.

 HE **TORAH** REPRESENTS THE FIRST FIVE BOOKS OF THE Bible. It tells the history of the human race from Creation through the founding of the Jewish nation and their settlement in the land of Israel.

God created the human race to be his pets. As a first-time pet owner, God wisely chose to start small, creating just two people: Adam and Eve. But, much like baby alligators, they proved to be rotten pets and were thus flushed into the sewer, where they propagated, until the sewers were overflowing with wild humans, hissing and spitting, fornicating and worshiping idols. So God flushed again. This time with a mighty flood.

When the survivors of the flood dried themselves off and re-populated the Earth, God decided that, rather than exterminating them, he would take another crack at domesticating human beings. Again, he decided to start small, with one family, the family of Abraham, whom he found to be smart and highly trainable. God gave Abraham and his descendants a set of laws with which to housebreak them. Then God found them a good home, a Promised Land where they could set a good example for the rest of the human race of how God envisioned this whole pet-thing playing out going forward.

In truth, though, God "discovered" the Promised Land in much the same way that my mother discovered the Olive Garden. Everybody already knew about it, and it was already full of people when she got there, but whatever, unlimited breadsticks!

When the Jews arrived at the Promised Land, they were a little irked to find the place overrun with pagans. The Promised Land was populated by many different tribes, each with their own unique culture and way of life. There were the Canaanites, the Amorites, the Girgashites… for our purposes, let's call them "Indians."

Whenever the Jews won a battle against the Indians, God ordered them to celebrate by killing all the men, women and children. He also ordered them to kill their cattle and their sheep and throw all their belongings into a bonfire, as if the Indians never existed. So it was sort of like, "You know, maybe we really *did* discover the Olive Garden."

When they were done clearing out all the pagans and their furniture, they named their new country "Israel," but this is not the end of the story. Being God's chosen people is always a roller-coaster ride…and this ride was just beginning.

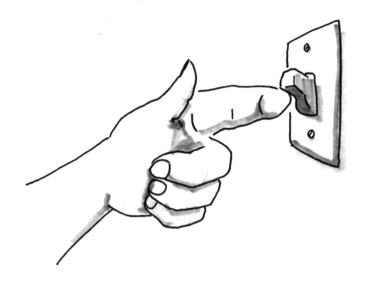

GENESIS

 N THE BEGINNING, God was lonely. So, he made the same mistake as a lot of men who live alone: he decided to go out and meet people. Only there weren't any people, so he had to make his own. God created Adam and Eve to be his friends.

God built a beautiful garden in Iraq for Adam and Eve to live in. Adam and Eve spent their days running around naked and playing Frisbee. They ate a lot of fruit. It was a lot like living at a Grateful Dead concert. God's one rule was that they couldn't eat the fruit from this magical tree he'd planted in the center of the garden.

I don't know why he put it there. It just tied the whole garden together.

Understandably, Adam and Eve were consumed with curiosity about this magical tree. It was just one of thousands of trees in the garden, but now they found it impossible to resist eating its fruit…and having a talking snake constantly goading them didn't help any. So Adam and Eve ate the fruit from the forbidden tree and were immediately endowed with the knowledge of good and evil, which mostly made them uptight about nudity.

When God found out about the missing fruit, he went apeshit.

"You need to stop playing the 'blame game.'"

He yelled at them, evicted Adam and Eve from the garden, and as extra punishment, he ordered them to become parents. This move really backfired, however, because Adam and Eve simply filled the world with children who murdered each other, worshiped idols and had sex with giants, all of which really dicked up God's plan for the earth.

God was so angry that he killed off the entire human race with a giant flood. Well, not the whole human race. He gave one guy named Noah a heads-up. Before the flood, Noah built an enormous boat and filled it with every species of animal he could find, which made Noah not only the world's first sailor, but its first animal hoarder as well. As soon as he finished packing the boat, the flood began. After forty days and nights of rain and a meat-heavy diet, the water subsided and Noah found land. When God saw the millions of dead bodies littering the ground, he wondered if maybe he'd overreacted.

So God wanted to make it right. But what could he do? What could possibly make up for killing nearly every living thing on the planet? Finally, it occurred to him. Everyone loves rainbows, right? He created this really sweet rainbow as a promise to never flood the Earth again.

But the moment Noah got back on dry land, he got drunk, and the human race just went right back to disappointing God.

God eventually found someone else he liked, though. God took a shine to a 75 year-old man named Abraham. God told Abraham that, even though he and his 90 year-old wife Sara were childless, he wanted to build a great nation out of them, and that Abraham's descendants would be his chosen people. To seal the deal, Abraham agreed to cut a tiny bit off the penis of every man who would ever be born into his family. Contracts worked differently back then.

Abraham went out into the wilderness to start his new nation. His nephew Lot tagged along, but he developed a taste for city living and left Abraham, moving his family to the twin cities of Sodom and Gomorrah.

God really hated Sodom and Gomorrah. The people there wanted to have sex with absolutely everything. They even tried to have sex with two angels God sent to warn Lot to leave town. Angel rape is not how you get on God's good side. So God incinerated the cities and all their inhabitants with fire and brimstone, except for Lot and his family, whom he let escape. But during their getaway,

Lot's wife made the mistake of turning to look back upon her burning hometown, for which God turned her into a pillar of salt, her punishment for the crime of nostalgia.

Lot's daughters felt it was a shame that, because their mother was salt, Lot would never have a son to carry on his family name. So they got their father drunk and had sex with him until he impregnated them both, which sort of made Lot his own father-in-law.

Abraham, meanwhile, was now in his nineties, and his wife Sarah was no spring chicken, either. To date, their geriatric sex had produced nothing but loads of dislocated hips and swollen ankles. Still, God insisted that he would build a great nation out of them. But Sarah told Abraham to sleep with her maid, so he could at least have some backup kids in case God's promise didn't pan out. Abraham did as he was told and slept with Hagar, who soon gave birth to a son named Ishmael. Abraham celebrated with free circumcisions for everybody.

Abraham's nontraditional family plugged along perfectly well until, against all odds, Sarah got pregnant. Abraham had finally produced a legitimate heir, whom they named Isaac. No longer needing a Plan B,

Sarah made Abraham get rid of Hagar and their son Ishmael.

Sadly, Abraham loaded them up with snacks and water and sent them out into the desert. Abraham would never see his son Ishmael again. But he took consolation in the fact that he had Isaac back at home and God had finally fulfilled his promise.

But then late one night, God woke Abraham up and ordered him to tie Isaac to an altar and to kill him as a human sacrifice, which apparently is the sort of thing God only does to people he likes.

Distraught with grief, Abraham nonetheless did what he was told. He took Isaac to the top of the mountain and tied him to the stone altar, but just when he was about to plunge his sacrificing knife into Isaac's chest, God stopped him. Turns out it was all a test of faith, or a really vicious prank, depending on how you look at it. Abraham had chosen God's need for a midnight snack over his son's life, and that was all the proof God needed that this was the family for him—his chosen people.

After his narrow escape from the aborted human sacrifice, Isaac grew up to be a man and had a couple of sons of his own, named Esau and Jacob. Jacob was a bit of a sugar-foot, staying at home with mom, helping her cook and clean and bake pies. Esau, on the other hand, was far more butch. He was a hunter, an outdoorsman, and as hairy as Burt Reynolds.

Esau was so hairy that Jacob tricked their father into giving him Esau's inheritance simply by covering himself in wool. After pulling off this act of identity theft, though, Jacob was forced to lay low for several years, evading his cheated brother. On the run, Jacob came to a farm and asked if he could stay there for a while.

"You can stay here," the farmer said. "Just don't be messin' with my two daughters."

But Jacob fell in love with his daughter Rachel, and offered to work the farm for seven years in exchange for being able to marry her. After seven years passed, the crafty farmer tricked him into marrying his older daughter, Leah.

"But I wanted to marry Rachel," he complained.

"That's fine," the farmer replied. "You can marry her, too. You just gotta work the farm for another seven years."

Jacob spent fourteen years working that guy's farm. His real rock bottom moment, though, came when he broke his arm wrestling with an angel. God changed Jacob's name to "Israel," which means "one who wrestles with God." As far as I know, Israel is still the only nation named after a wrestler.

Israel and his two wives had twelve sons, one of whom was named Joseph. The other sons mostly hated Joseph and it's hard to blame them. Joseph was clearly the favorite, was always getting the best presents from their dad, and he wasted no opportunity to remind his brothers of this fact. When he told his brothers about a dream where they were all bowing down to him, this really sent them over the edge. They threw Joseph into a pit and sold him as a slave.

"That ought to take him down a peg," they said as the slave caravan disappeared into the distance.

But it turns out that Joseph really was better than everybody else. He was taken to Egypt as a penniless slave and within a few years, he was practically running the place. The Pharaoh had a disturbing dream in which seven plump cows emerged from the Nile and devoured seven skinny cows. Joseph explained that this meant that Egypt would have seven years of bumper crops, followed by seven years of famine. The Pharaoh put Joseph in charge of the Department of Agriculture and due to his unorthodox strategy of planning the Egyptian economy around the Pharaoh's dreams, Egypt was spared from a horrible famine.

Not one to hold a grudge, Joseph wrote to his brothers, telling them to come live in Egypt where he was a big shot and they'd have plenty to eat. The dream had come true. His brothers would be bowing down to him, after all. As humiliating as that was, though, it was less embarrassing than starving to death. So the brothers packed up and moved to Egypt and the descendants of the twelve brothers would go on to become the twelve tribes of Israel.

God had made a nation out of Abraham's ninety-year old loins. Now even when he got disgusted with the human race, there would still be one group of people he could hang out with.

"A few friends I can count on," God told himself. "That's all I need."

EXODUS

WHEN THE **PHARAOH** saw all these Israelites living in Egypt, he thought, "Holy shit! We've got an illegal alien problem."

So the Pharaoh enslaved God's chosen people and put them to work picking green beans, framing houses, and things like that. Not wanting her son to grow up as a slave, one lady put her baby in straw basket and released it into the Nile River. The Pharaoh's daughter stumbled upon the basket while she was out swimming. She later adopted the boy and named him Moses.

As Moses grew up, he went to the best schools, ate the best food, played with the best dogs, and generally lived the good life. All of which was built on the misery of an army of slaves. But then one day he learned the awful truth: he wasn't a blue-blooded Egyptian at all. In fact, he was the son of illegal aliens. Having learned of how he came to be in the Pharaoh's family, it occurred to Moses that the only thing that separated him from the slaves being whipped outside the palace was a basket ride. This realization caused an existential crisis in Moses.

He turned his back on his adopted family, his country club, and all his yuppie friends, and went into the desert to sort things out.

While in the desert, God appeared to Moses in the form of a burning bush and told him to go free his fellow Israelites from slavery. Now, when a flaming shrub tells you to do something, you do it.

Moses returned to Egypt, demanding the release of all the Israelite slaves. The Pharaoh thought his radicalized grandson was just going through a phase. That if he just held out long enough, Moses would shave off his beard and the Che Guevara poster would come down off the wall, and everything would go back to normal. But Moses was serious, and so was God, a point he drove home by turning the Nile River into blood, creating swarms of frogs and giving everyone skin boils. In light of these horrors, the Pharaoh offered to let the Israelites go, but only if they left their cattle and sheep behind. This wasn't good enough for Moses, as he knew this meant a future without jerky or leather furniture. So to raise the stakes, Moses summoned the Angel of Death.

That night, the Israelites covered their door frames with lamb's blood, so the Angel of Death would know to pass over their house and to move on to the neighbors, where he would kill their first-born son. This is where the Jewish Feast of Passover comes from.

The Israelites got to keep their sheep and cattle. And they got to leave Egypt. God told Moses to take his people into the desert and await further instructions.

The Egyptians had made running a government look easy, but Moses quickly learned that it's actually kind of a grind, especially when you're leading a nation of people on what is going to be a 40-year nature hike.

There was simply no way Moses could be everywhere to make sure nobody killed anyone else, stole their food, screwed their wife, or ate something that made them sick. And even when he could catch someone in the act, there wasn't much he could do about it. You can't exactly put someone in jail when you're marching ten miles a day.

Moses did his best to keep order, but people kept getting sick, fights would break out and people were so fed up with the situation that they threatened to leave and go back to Egypt. For a while, it looked as if in the midst of all this crime and chaos that the tribes of Israel might simply dissolve and everyone would go their separate ways.

Moses wracked his brain for ways to keep his nation of hikers together. Finally, God decided to help Moses out. He called him up to the top of Mount Sinai and gave him a bunch of stone tablets. "Be sure to tell everyone that these are coming from me." God told him. "If they follow these laws, I'll always be there to watch over them," God said. "That's the deal." To commemorate his deal with the people of Israel, God told Moses to build the Ark of the Covenant, a gold trunk decorated with angels. Inside the trunk, they kept the Ten Commandments and some other mementos. They also built a Mercy Seat, a little seat on top of the ark so that when he came down from Heaven, God could ride around on top and kill people as they carried the ark with them.

After a few days, Moses came back down the mountain with a bunch of laws, and unlike the rules he'd tried to lay down, these laws, he told them, were given to him personally by God. A gasp went up from the crowd. This was serious poker. People were far more worried about disobeying God who, unlike Moses, actually *could* be everywhere at once. So they cut down on cheating, robbing, and killing each other and generally cleaned up their act.

The nation of hikers was saved.

LEVITICUS

To: The children of Israel
From: Moses
Re: A Few New Rules

ow that we aren't in Egypt anymore, we're going to need our own laws. Luckily, during our get-together on Mount Sinai, God gave me 613 easy-to-follow rules. To sum up:

First off, God wants you to make sacrifices to him. If you've sinned, if you've just had a baby, or if you just want to make God feel special, you can bring him goats, sheep, cows, little cakes. You know, that sort of thing. If you're going to make a sacrifice, though, it's got to be primo stuff. No three-legged goats or burnt bread.

Speaking of food— starting now, you all have to eat kosher. What does "kosher" mean? Well, it basically means there's certain things you can't eat. No bats and no wild birds. You have no idea what those birds are up to when they're out flying around. No lizards (sorry, Simon the Lizard-Eater, I know this one's especially hard on you). Fish are cool, as long as they have scales and fins. Eels and shellfish

are just…I don't know, sort of gross. You can eat any animal that has cleft hooves, EXCEPT for pigs, camels and badgers. Don't ask me why you can't eat badgers, you just can't. Insects that fly are out, but insects that walk on the ground are okay. You can eat all the termites you want.

If you have a mildew problem, you have to burn your clothes and blankets. If you have a wet dream, you have to take a bath. If you have a pus-filled sore, take a bath and then burn your clothes. If someone gets a skin disease, make him take a bath and shave off all his hair. If a man with eczema spits on you, you have to take a bath and burn all your clothes. If we can't be the holiest people of all time, we'll damn well be the cleanest.

God has Ten Commandments which he thinks are REALLY important. They are as follows:

I. No other gods (at least not that you like better than God).

II. No idols. That's sort of like expecting your wife to be okay with keeping a picture of your ex-girlfriend on your desk.

III. No invoking God's name in vain. If you're going to start a fight, leave God out of it.

IV. Keep the Sabbath. No working on Saturdays. Everyone needs at least one day off.

V. Don't embarrass mom and dad Trust me, this one will come in handy when you have kids of your own.

VI. Don't kill each other. I would have hoped this one would be obvious.

VII. No adultery. Everybody sleep in your own tent.

VIII. Don't steal. What's mine ISN'T yours.

IX. Don't lie about each other, or falsely accuse each other of crimes. Don't make us look stupid for punishing the wrong guy. And finally...

X. Don't get jealous over each other's shit. None of you really have anything worth being jealous over, anyway. I don't care how nice your neighbor's shepherd staff is, it shouldn't keep you awake at night.

In addition, God forbids the following: club sandwiches, gay sex between men, sorcery, incest, making fun of the deaf, bestiality, shaving, tattoos, rare steaks, gossip, cotton-and-wool twills, threesomes, crooked scales, sex with slaves, and eating animals if you don't know how they died.

God also gave me several penalties for breaking these laws, most of which are rather unpleasant, and frankly, complicated. For example, if a couple commits good old-fashioned adultery, they're both to be killed. But if a guy complicates matters by sleeping with his wife's mother, then all three of them have to be burned to death, including the wife, who might not have even known what was going on. Harsh, I know.

If a man has sex with his wife while she is on her period, then they're merely exiled. But if a man has sex with an animal, both he and the animal have to be killed. And just so you know, if the nation as a whole ignores these laws, then your crops will be eaten by invaders and your children will be devoured by wild animals. So there's no safety in numbers here.

If you have any questions about these laws, take them up with the priests. Oh, and priests, we've got a few rules for you, too. First of all, keep your hair looking nice. God likes that. And make sure you use the right kind of oil in your ceremonies. You have to be very careful about sacrifices. You know my brother Aaron? His sons Nadab and Adihu used the wrong oil in a sacrifice and God killed them right there on the spot. So needless to say, this is a no-bullshit business. Also, priests, you have to marry virgins. Oh, and no amputees. They have no relationship with God.

Okay, those are the laws God gave me to pass on to you. Isn't this exciting?

"God just sent down more rules: no gays, no tattoos, and no ham sandwiches."

NUMBERS

OD DECIDED TO channel his anger into more positive activities, like hobbies. It was around this time that God got bit by the real estate bug. He found this great piece of beach front property on the Mediterranean and thought it would be just perfect for his chosen people, so he gave it to them. Which is sort of like me giving you Gary's sandwich out of the break room fridge. Despite being promised to them, the land already belonged to other people. So, if the Israelites wanted their Promised Land, they would have to conquer it themselves.

Moses took a census of all the tribes and drafted an army. One of the problems with going to war is that while the men are away fighting, the women tend to get lonely. So Moses came up with a method for testing whether a wife was cheating on her husband.

It went like this: The priests would put a curse on some water, and have the wife drink it. If she had remained faithful, nothing would happen to her. But if she'd been sleeping around, she would get really fat and her thighs would rot off. It's not clear whether this was actually expected to work, or if it was just something Moses came up with to put the minds of nervous husbands at ease.

With their army assembled, and their test for wayward wives in hand, the nation of Israel marched towards the Promised Land. At first, they were fresh and happy, blowing their trumpets, showing off the Ark of the Covenant, waving to people in the desert as they passed by.

After a while, though, they started getting cranky. They complained about having nothing to eat but the bread that God magically laid out on the ground for them every night. They fantasized about the fish, cucumbers, and melons they used to eat back in Egypt. They griped to Moses. If God could send them magic bread, couldn't he just as easily summon up a falafel wrap or some meat?

This ingratitude really chafed God. "Oh, they want meat, do they?" he said spitefully, "I'll give them some meat!" God sent wave after wave of quails crashing into the ground until everyone was wading

*"I don't care if we're lost.
I'm not asking for directions."*

up to their waists in dead birds. Despite all the quail meat, though, people kept complaining.

Moses sent a scouting team ahead of the nation of hikers to check out the Promised Land. The scouts reported that, on the plus side, it was a veritable "land of milk and honey." The scouts were less enthusiastic, however, about the fact that the land was populated by angry giants. Of all the scouts, only two, Joshua and Caleb, recommended going forward. People weren't eager to fight these giants, though. Moaning turned into panic and people began speaking openly of revolt and returning to Egypt.

Even Moses' sister Miriam questioned his judgment in forging ahead into this terrifying new land.

Now, there are few things God hates more than a whiner. As punishment for her complaining, God gave Miriam leprosy for seven days. Everyone else got snakes.

Poisonous snakes started popping up out of nowhere, biting people left and right. When God felt that the whiners had enough, he told Moses to build a pole with a brass snake winding around it. When the people quit their grumbling and looked up at the pole, all their snakebites were magically cured. The pole with snakes went on to become our symbol for medicine. You can still see it on the side of ambulances today, even though they rarely get called out for mass snakebites.

Wherever they went, tens of thousands of Israelites would suddenly show up uninvited, trampling the grass, devouring the crops, and drinking everything in sight. They were like a plague of locusts or hippies.

Soon, the hikers of Israel encountered the Midianites and their slutty women. Their sluttiness infuriated God, as they were always seducing the Israelite men. So God told Moses to send the army to slaughter the Midianites. The soldiers went in and killed all the Midianite men. But when Moses showed up and saw the mountain of bodies, he wasn't happy at all.

"I told you to kill ALL the Midianites. Why are there still all these women and children standing around?" The soldiers objected to killing unarmed women and children, but Moses coaxed them into it by letting them each keep one virgin girl as a souvenir.

On that sour note, the Israelites at last arrived at the River Jordan. Across the river lay the Promised Land. Moses died before they could cross the river, though, leaving Joshua in charge. Joshua was the kind of guy who didn't get squeamish at the sight of blood, and that was a good thing because the killing had just begun.

DEUTERONOMY

JUST BEFORE HE DIED, Moses said, "I won't be around to see it, but you're all about to come into a whole lot of land. When that happens you will no longer be a traveling group of tribes but a bona fide nation. So, as a parting gift, I wanted to give you a few hundred extra laws to help you along. Everybody ready? Okay, here we go:

"Guys, don't marry foreign girls and don't rape any girls, foreign or not. If you rape somebody and they are engaged to be married, then your punishment is to be stoned to death. If you rape somebody and they're *not* engaged to be married, then your punishment is to marry her.

"If two guys are fighting in the street and one of their wives jumps in and grabs the other guy's balls, cut off her hand. The last thing we need around here is a nut-clutcher.

"Once you get around to building towns and cities, set aside three cities as places of refuge. If you accidentally kill somebody and their relatives come looking for you, try to make it to one of these three cities. Once you're inside a city of refuge, they have to let you stay and no one can kill you.

"I wish he'd hurry up and die. He keeps making more laws."

If you kill somebody on purpose, however, you're on your own.

"If you get married and for some reason you think that your wife is not a virgin, you can take it up with the elders. If it turns out that you're right, you can have her stoned to death. But if it turns out that you're wrong, then you have to pay her father a hundred shekels for slandering the merchandise.

"Build a fence around your roof so that no one will fall off while you're up there. It may seem silly now, but trust me, this will save you a lot of grief in the long run.

"If you're a soldier and you have a wet dream, you've got to leave camp for one whole day before you come back. Also, when you're in camp, be sure to shit discreetly in a hole. Remember, God walks among you, and the last thing you want is for him to be stepping in your shit.

"Don't take a man's tools as security for a debt. If you take his livelihood from him, how is he supposed to pay you back, dumbass? And if you take his cloak as collateral, give it back to him when night comes around so he doesn't freeze to death. Don't take advantage of the poor and don't be stingy. Once you go harvesting through your fields once, leave whatever's left over for widows and orphans. You don't need to squeeze every last grape out of your land. This shall be your social safety net.

"If you do these things and observe all the other laws I've given you, then God will lift you above all other nations. If you don't, then God will send a hairy foreigner to steal your girlfriend. If you have trouble remembering all these laws, then as a rule of thumb, treat each other well and you should be okay. And if God wants you to do something, don't ask too many questions, just do it, even if it's kind of weird."

And with that, Moses died.

"*I don't care what other people say. I like you.*"

PART TWO
THE HISTORY

In which people learn not to touch God's stuff, a series of handsome men become king, and God gets a new hobby.

HESE BOOKS TELL THE STORY OF THE RISE AND FALL OF THE nation of Israel: of how God's chosen people went from a loose affiliation of tribes ruled by amateur "judges," to a real nation with a king and everything. King Solomon would build God a massive temple, a sort of vacation home he could live in when he came down from Heaven to check in on his Chosen People. It would at once serve as a testament to their commitment to God, and proof to the world that theirs was not just a country of shepherds and hillbillies, but a legitimate civilization.

To make God's commute easier, they built the temple at the exact spot where they believed Heaven and Earth to meet. Then, once a year, everyone would come to the temple, sacrifice animals to God, and their best priest would enter God's private chamber, shake his hand, and apologize for anything the people might have done to offend him.

They had never been so close, God and his people, and yet the very thing that brought them together would tear them apart. The temple was so expensive and labor-intensive that Solomon was forced to pass a crushing bill on to his people to pay for it. To make matters worse, he didn't split the tab evenly, dumping most of it on the northern tribes. Not having the money or manpower to pay their bill, they decided instead to dine and dash. The northern tribes would split off into their own kingdom, dividing Israel into two weak kingdoms. And everything would go downhill from there.

JOSHUA

ITH **MOSES DEAD,** Joshua became the new leader of the Israelites. He knew that if he was going to conquer Canaan with an army of hikers, he was going to need a fair amount of divine intervention. When the time came to ask for God's help, the last thing he needed was for God to be turned off by the sight of uncircumcised dongs. So Joshua gathered all the men who'd made it through the desert *au naturel* at the "Hill of Foreskins" and ordered a fresh round of circumcisions.

They sent spies ahead to see what awaited them. The spies soon came to a town called Jericho, the oldest city in the world. The fortifications of Jericho were so high and thick that whole shops, apartments, and brothels fit inside the wall. When the spies got inside Jericho's wall, they made a beeline past the apartments and the wall-marts to the whorehouse, where they were taken in by a prostitute named Rahab, who agreed to hide the spies if the Israelites would take care of her when they conquered the city.

Not long after, the cops showed up at Rahab's door and asked if they could look around. "We got a report of some suspicious characters lurking around here."

"This is a brothel," she said, "we only get suspicious characters around here."

"These guys were foreigners. They wore tassels and smelled like sheep. They were missing a piece off their dicks. You notice anyone like that?"

"Oh yeah, those guys were here, all right. They already left, though."

"Are you sure? They were seen here only about an hour ago."

"Most of my guests don't stay more than ten minutes," Rahab said.

This story seemed to capture the cops' imagination, so they left Rahab alone.

The spies returned to tell Joshua how high and thick the city walls were, and how cool Rahab the prostitute had been to them.

God surveyed the situation from his perch atop the Ark of the Covenant. Rather than attack Jericho's walls in a frontal assault,

"I'll teach you to make fun of my horn."

God ordered Joshua to take advantage of his people's natural hiking ability, marching them in circles around the city once a day for six days in a row. On the seventh day, they had to march around the city seven times. After completing all their laps around Jericho, the priests blew their trumpets, and all the soldiers screamed as hard as they could, which caused the city's walls to collapse. Only the wall brothel was left standing. Joshua and his soldiers rushed in and killed every man, woman, and child in the city.

Jericho was destroyed, and just like that, six thousand years of civilization had come to an end. As if it weren't enough that the city had been obliterated,

Joshua ordered his army to hand the spoils over to the priests and bury the ruins. He left no trace of the city's existence, and threatened to kill the children of anyone who attempted to rebuild the city. Some people are just sore winners.

Rahab and her family were spared. In exchange for her treason, she was absorbed into the nation of Israel, and would go on to become the matriarch of quite an impressive family tree. King David, King Solomon and Jesus Christ would all someday be the descendants of Rahab, the helpful hooker.

Next they attacked the diminutive town of Ai. Joshua figured that after taking down the oldest city in the world, Ai would be easy pickings. But the army of Ai led Joshua's soldiers into an ambush and routed them. Joshua concluded that the loss could not possibly be because of any failure of leadership on his part, but rather that someone must have angered God by keeping some cups or plates from the Battle of Jericho.

A man named Achen was eventually singled out, and he admitted to having taken some silver coins, a slab of gold and a fetching robe out of Jericho. Joshua had Achen, his belongings, his children, his cattle, and even the stuff he'd looted dumped into a big pile at the bottom of a valley. There, they were all stoned to death and their remains were burned. Joshua didn't have any problems with looters after that.

Under Joshua's no-nonsense style of leadership, the Israelites went on to conquer the Promised Land, city by city. Having an Ark of the Covenant to shoot death rays everywhere didn't hurt, either.

Joshua then split up the new land among the twelve tribes. The Israelites finally had a land they could call Israel. As he lay on his deathbed, Joshua summoned the whole nation before him.

"What a long, strange trip it's been," he said. "From the time God told Abraham to build a nation, and that whole enslavement thing in Egypt, to the forty years we spent wandering through the wilderness. But now, at last, we've done it. We've built ourselves a new home. Try not to blow it after I'm gone."

Having given his farewell address, Joshua died.

JUDGES

 PPARENTLY, JOSHUA'S "mission accomplished" speech was a tad premature.

The Promised Land was still rotten with heathens, and without a strong leader like Joshua running the army, it wasn't long before bigger nations started carving off pieces of the fledgling nation for themselves.

Eglon, the morbidly obese King of the Moabites, began extorting the nation of Israel for tribute. The Israelites sent a messenger named Ehud to take Eglon his protection money. Ehud asked if he could speak to the king privately. When the two ducked into a side room, instead of giving him the money, Ehud unsheathed a sword and sunk the blade into the abundant gut of the king. The servants, assuming that Eglon had slipped out to take one of his notoriously huge shits, didn't bother checking up on him. When they finally found his dead body, they couldn't pull the sword out because it was stuck in all his gut-fat.

By the time Ehud returned to Israel, he had become a national hero. They made Ehud their "judge," or the person who would rule them on God's behalf.

But Israel's respite from foreign domination was short-lived. After Ehud died, the Hazorites started squeezing Israel. The new judge, Deborah, the only woman to ever be a Judge of Israel, raised an army to fight them off. But Deborah's soldiers were armed with nothing but a bunch of ramshackle bronze swords and spears. The Hazorites, on the other hand, were heavily armed with the latest, state-of-the-art war technology, including helmets, metal body armor, and chariots. The night before their battle, Deborah led her army to the top of a mountain. It seemed like a simple matter of time before the Hazorites found Deborah's army and destroyed them. But the next morning, Deborah shrewdly launched a surprise attack, pouring down the east face of the mountain at sunrise. When the Hazorites looked up to defend themselves, they were blinded by the rising sun. Sunglasses hadn't been invented yet.

In addition, the Hazorites' chariots were useless in the soft, dewy morning mud. In this muddy, chaotic combat, their heavy expensive armor just weighed them down, while the light, dollar-store weaponry of the Israelites allowed them to maneuver nimbly, hacking off the arms and heads of their mud-bound enemies.

In the upset of the year, the Israelites routed the Hazorites. The general in charge of the Hazorite army fled the battle, and holed up in a nearby farmer's tent. While hiding, he asked the farmer's wife to bring him something to drink. She served her guest a glass of warm milk, which was highly approved of as an act of hospitality in those days. But then, after he fell asleep, she drove a tent peg through his skull, which was generally frowned upon as poor customer service.

After Deborah's victory, there was peace for forty years, until Israel was invaded by the Midianites, whose inherent sluttiness apparently helped them rebound nicely from the genocide Moses tried on them.

"I suppose this means they'll be needing my help again," God sighed. God approached a man named Gideon and asked him to raise an army to defend Israel. "Don't worry," God told him, "You'll be marvelous. I'll be right there with you the whole time."

"My stupid sword is stuck in your stupid fat."

So Gideon set up a recruiting station and started visiting local high schools. Before long, he'd talked thirty thousand guys into joining his army. "You did a good job recruiting," God told him, "but if you go into battle with that army, you're going to get slaughtered."

"Why? What's wrong with my army?"

"Well, for one thing, it's way too big. What's more, it's filled with goose-bumpy farmers who'll shit their loincloth the second things get real. Here's what I want you to do: tell everyone who's afraid they can go home."

"But that's everybody!" Gideon complained. Nevertheless, Gideon agreed to release anyone who'd been taken in by the recruiting posters and cool uniforms and two-thirds of them left.

"Hey. Hey, Gideon," God said.

"What?" Gideon replied miffed.

"You're totally going to hate me, but your army's still too big." As Gideon sat there wondering what he'd got himself into, God told him to pick his army by watching how his men drank water from a stream.

"Send anyone home who doesn't lap the water like a dog. Trust me, you want those dog-lappers.

You can sneak up on guys who stick their whole head into the water. But you ever sneak up on a dog?"

Gideon nervously watched his men drink from the stream and just about fainted when only a few hundred guys turned out to be lappers.

Gideon was left with more of a Boy Scout troop than an army. With only three hundred men, fighting a traditional battle was out of the question. But the advantage of having so few men was that they could move around quickly and quietly. He could maneuver them undetected at night and take them on field trips. Gideon discovered that he could sneak his entire force right up to the Midianite camp without anyone noticing.

The Midianites were all fast asleep or jerking off in their tents when they were woken up by a loud trumpet blast. They got out of bed to find themselves being ambushed. The Midianites fumbled for their weapons. They panicked, stabbed each other in the dark, and ran away half-dressed into the night, assuming they'd been attacked by a huge army.

After his victory over the Midianites, the people offered to make

Gideon a judge, but he decided that he didn't really like this kind of work. He asked for one gold earring from every man in Israel as payment for his services, and retired.

Also among the judges was Jephtah, son of Gilead. Jephtah was born poor tent park trash and was tough as nails. In a barroom brawl, he was unstoppable. But because his mother was a prostitute, the rest of his family kept him out of sight like an old pair of acid-washed jeans, until they became embroiled in a nasty land dispute with some foreigners. Knowing there was a fight coming, they turned to Jephtah and made him their leader.

Jephtah strapped on his headband and his leather vest. He mounted his low-rider camel and rode into battle. Jephtah laid a trucker-beating on the foreigners and returned home a champion. Jephtah was feeling so good that he swore to take the first thing he saw and burn it as an offering to God. As he rolled up into the tent park, he looked around for a sheep or a goat that might be milling around in the front yard. Instead, his front door flung open and his only daughter came running out to give him a hug.

When he saw his daughter running up to him, he burst into tears and tore his leather vest in grief. He told his daughter about the oath he'd made.

"Since you made a promise to God," she told him, "you can't back out, no matter how stupid it is. All I ask is that you give me two months to roam the hills and say goodbye to my friends."

Two months later, his daughter returned and was burned as a human sacrifice to God. This started a tradition where every year the girls of Israel leave home for four days to mourn the daughter of Jephtah.

Perhaps the most famous judge of all was Samson. He was sort of like the Jewish Hercules. God granted Samson supernatural strength on the condition that he never cut his hair. By this time, a tribe of seafaring merchants called the Philistines had taken over and were ruling Israel. Despite their name, the Philistines were actually a cultured, cosmopolitan people. They loved art and imported wine.

Samson fought the Philistines, but not really as a freedom fighter. He was more like a seventeen-year-old in a letterman's jacket, challenging the Philistines to a fight in the parking lot of a Burger King. He'd wander into town, beat up a bunch of random Philistines, and later when their buddies

"Just a trim."

cornered him at a whorehouse, he not only clobbered the guys who came to get revenge on him, but he tore the city gates off their hinges and carried them off as a prank.

Samson also had a thing for hot Philistine women. He married a Philistine, then threw her out of the house after she cost him a bet. Nor was Samson a very gracious ex-husband. When she remarried, Samson's wedding present to her was to take 300 foxes, light their tails on fire and set them loose in the wheat fields, destroying the Philistine's crops. After that, about a thousand Philistines showed up at Samson's house spoiling for a fight, but Samson killed them all with the jawbone of a donkey which was conveniently laying nearby.

Despite the flop that was his first marriage, Samson fell for another Philistine, named Delilah. Delilah was the kind of trouble that wears a name tag. Once married, she immediately started pestering Samson into telling her the secret behind his enormous strength. He lied, telling her that if he was tied up with new rope that he would become as weak as a baby.

While he slept, Delilah tied him up with rope. Then she let the Philistines in to the house. They poured in to beat Samson into submission. But to Samson, their tiny little fists felt as if he were being pummeled by a declawed cat.

"Oh, isn't that cute?" he said, rousing from his sleep. Then he tore through the ropes like cobwebs and demolished the Philistines with his bare hands.

Despite obvious trust issues in their marriage, everything seemed to go back to normal for Samson and Delilah. And it wasn't long before Delilah was again nagging him to tell her what made him so strong. Finally, Samson caved in and told her that his strength came from his long, beautiful, Michael Landon-esque hair.

That night, Delilah shaved Samson's head while he slept. Apparently, Samson was a heavy sleeper. At last, the Philistines were able to storm the house and arrest bald Sampson without being killed by fists or animal parts. Not wanting to take any chances, the Philistines

gouged out Samson's eyes and threw him in a dungeon.

Many years later, the King of the Philistines was having a big celebration and thought it might be fun to trot Samson out as a party favor. They fished Samson out of the dungeon and stood him between the center pillars of the palace so everyone could get a good look at him. What they had failed to notice, however, was the fact that Samson's hair had grown back.

Standing there, amongst the shrimp cocktails and mushroom appe-teasers, Samson regretted wasting so much of his youth and taking for granted the enormous power God had given him. Samson asked God to give him his strength back one more time so that he could finally do something useful with his life.

Blind and chained, Samson's biceps swelled and he felt the old rush of adrenaline he had known as a young man. He reached out, grasped the pillars, and pulled them down with all his might, killing himself, the Philistine king, the cocktail servers, and everyone at the party. Through the power of hair, God had toppled the Philistine government liberating the Israelites once again.

RUTH

 UTH BEGINS WITH the marriage of an Israelite man to a foreign woman named Naomi. Naomi gave birth to two sons, who themselves married foreign girls, a pair of Moabites named Orpah and Ruth. Life was good for Naomi's extended family until all three husbands died in quick succession, leaving the women in a precarious situation. In those days, a woman's financial security depended completely on having a man around who could work the land, sell the crops and father loads of sons to do the same. Naomi inherited a tiny plot of land, but found herself without a husband or sons and too old to get more of either. Things looked pretty grim for Naomi.

Realizing that her life had become a tragedy in waiting, Naomi told Orpah and Ruth to leave her and to return to their families in Moab. Orpah didn't need to be told twice; without missing a beat, she caught the next camel back home. But Ruth couldn't bring herself to leave her mother-in-law to starve or be eaten by coyotes or whatever became of old widows in those days.

So Ruth and Naomi braced themselves for the hardscrabble existence of a couple of homeless women. They got most of their food from the welfare system Moses had created. That is to say, she worked as a gleaner, one of the people who picked through a field after it had already been harvested in order to get whatever crops had

"Orpah, not Oprah.
Everyone makes that mistake."

been left behind. Whatever she could scrape together from the fields was what she and Naomi would have to live on.

One day, the landlord was out supervising the harvest when he saw this young beauty in the fields, picking leftovers along with the cripples, drunks and other castoffs of Hebrew society. Intrigued, the landlord did a little snooping, and when he heard how Ruth had heroically chosen to care for her mother-in-law, he was so moved that he called her over to him.

"My name is Boaz," he said. "Look, I don't want you working out there in the fields with all the snakes and weeds," he said, "why don't you stay here by the tents and work with my other female employees? There's plenty of water for when you get thirsty and this way the farmhands won't hit on you."

After work, when Ruth told her about this fortuitous development, Naomi's eyes lit up. Naomi smelled a golden opportunity for Ruth to snag a new husband. And having been around the block a few times, Naomi knew just how to seal the deal.

"The first thing you got to do," she told Ruth, "is take a bath. Do you have any perfume? Can you make some out of these beets and cauliflower you brought home? Men like a sweet-smelling woman. Okay, when you go to work tomorrow, be sure to wear something flattering."

"I can't work in a tight fitting dress," Ruth protested.

"I don't care if you can work in it or not. You're trying to win a man here, not 'Beet-Picker of the Year.' After work, find out where he's sleeping. Go in there, reach under his blanket and dig around with your hand until you find the buried treasure. It's that simple. He'll take it from there."

"I don't know…"

"Oh, come on!" Naomi reassured her. "A little trouser fishing never hurt anyone! It's how the game is played! Do you want to eat secondhand cauliflower the rest of your life?"

The next day, Ruth reluctantly took her mother-in-law's advice. Ruth found Boaz alone in the threshing room. She hid in there, secretly watching Boaz threshing barley and dripping with sweat, his shirt off and arms glistening. Then, after finishing his work, Boaz enjoyed a little nightcap and laid down to rest. This was her cue. Once he was asleep, Ruth crept in and peeled the blanket

"Guess who's too good to work in the fields now that she's sleeping with the boss?"

back. Boaz woke with a jolt to find himself naked, and there, among the sweaty barley and perfume, Ruth kneeling down beside him.

"Ruth, I've wanted you since the moment I first saw you in the fields," Boaz said. "I think you're the greatest woman I've ever met. And I want you to be my wife. But there's rules for this sort of thing. My people live according to the Laws of Moses, and holy shit, did that guy have a lot of laws. One of his laws being that when a woman is widowed, her dead husband's closest male relative gets first crack at marrying her.

According to the law, before I can marry you, I have to find this guy and offer you to him. I don't want to, but I have to."

"So, do you want me to leave?" Ruth asked.

"Now, I didn't say THAT," Boaz replied.

The two spent the night together on the threshing floor. The next morning, Ruth got up really early because she didn't want anyone to see her scurrying away with her hair matted and dress askew.

Now, Boaz wanted to marry Ruth, but he knew that she was so beautiful that if he simply offered her to another man, there was a good chance he'd take him up on it. So Boaz hatched a little plan: he put Naomi's small piece of land up for sale. Boaz then summoned the relative, telling him that he had some land to sell him. Boaz told the man how lush and fertile the land was, and then, to really sweeten the pot, he offered him a rock bottom price. The guy jumped at the offer.

Now, in ancient Israel, no deal was final until the buyer and seller swapped sandals. That way if someone tried to back out of it later, the other guy could produce his sandal in court and the judge would say, "If you didn't have an agreement, how did he get your sandal?" at which point you'd either have to admit that you made a deal or that you were too much of a marshmallow to keep someone from knocking you over and taking your shoes. Either way, the law was not on your side.

Anyway, just before the two men were about to swap sandals, Boaz nonchalantly added, "Oh, by the way, I don't know if I mentioned this earlier, but whoever buys this old lady's land also has to marry her widowed daughter-in-law."

This shady fine print immediately sent the buyer into red alert.

"Wait, what was that last bit?"

Boaz mumbled the part about marrying Ruth again. The man said. "Oh, I see what's going on here, you're trying to unload some old maid on me. I was wondering why the price was so low. Thanks, but no thanks. Tell you what, if it's such a great deal, then why don't YOU buy the land and marry the widow?"

Which is precisely what Boaz had in mind. Boaz and Ruth were married, Naomi moved in and soon the happy newlyweds had a baby, named Obed. Little Obed would go on to be the grandpa of King David. Like Rahab before her, Ruth would go on to become the maternal ancestor of the most famous family line in history. King David, King Solomon and Jesus Christ would not only be the descendants of a prostitute, but a homeless woman as well.

THE 1ˢᵀ BOOK OF SAMUEL

THE WHOLE ANCIENT world was a bag of dicks. Even God was a bit of a dick. Life was so cheap that nobody really held it against you if you killed a person or two. How could you avoid it? So mercy was pretty much out of the question. The best you could hope for was that people would honor their deals. And people were always trying to make a deal with God.

A woman named Hannah stumbled into the tabernacle one evening, weeping. Having no children, she begged God to give her a son. In exchange, she promised to dedicate her son to the priesthood. The high priest, Eli, came out to see what all the commotion was, assuming she was drunk, he shooed Hannah out of the tabernacle.

Her prayer worked, though. Hannah soon became pregnant. She named her child "Samuel,"

which means "God heard me." Honoring her end of the deal, Hannah took the boy to the tabernacle to make him a priest. Hannah went on to have many other babies. She just needed that first one to get the ball rolling.

Eli raised Samuel to be a priest. He had also trained his sons to be priests, but they weren't exactly cut out for that line of work. They were always sleeping with the tent-greeters and embezzling meat. In those days, when people brought an ox or a cow to sacrifice to God, the priests would burn it. They were allowed to stick a fork into the roasting beef, and whatever they could pull out was their tip. But Eli's sons juiced the game by carving up tenderloins and pot roasts until they were barely hanging on, allowing them to fork off the best cuts of meat for themselves. Basically, they were skimming from the till.

God is a picky eater, and the last thing you want to do is to steal his meat. God decided that Eli's sons had to go.

Israel had many enemies, but the Philistines were sort of like Israel's division rivalry. It wasn't long before the Philistines attacked Israel. It was *never* long before the Philistines attacked Israel.

Just as they had countless times before, Eli's sons hitched the Ark of the Covenant to its carrying poles and raced out to the battle so God could come out shooting death rays, killing their enemies, popping their organs, and burning off their faces, Raiders-of-the-Lost-Ark style.

Instead, though, the Ark did nothing. As the battle raged on, the Ark sat there motionless, like a jammed pistol in a gunfight. Without their secret weapon, the Israelites were routed by the Philistines. The Ark of the Covenant was taken as a war trophy. When Eli heard that his sons were dead and the Ark had been captured, he fell backwards out of his chair, broke his neck, and died.

At first, the Philistines gloated over having captured the Ark of the Covenant, on which rode the Israelites' cranky God. They put the Ark in their temple, so their god, Dagon, would have some company. The two did not get along. God complained about his living situation by giving the Philistines cancer and plagues of rats. The Philistines took the hint. They hitched the Ark to a team of oxen and sent it wandering back towards Israel. As a token of respect for a God who could summon such awful curses, they sent along a bag of commemorative gold figurines in the shape of little rats and tumors.

When the Israelites saw the oxen pulling the Ark back into town, they got excited.

"Hey look, the Ark's back!" they shouted. "Do you think it's still broken?" As if checking under the hood of a car, they opened the lid of the Ark and it promptly killed seventy people. "Nope. Seems to be working just fine!"

God was now free to start the priesthood over from scratch, preferably with someone who wouldn't tamper with his meat. Samuel succeeded Eli as the high priest of Israel. Samuel was a good man, but he made the mistake, so common to good men, of placing his trust in fools. In this case, his own sons, whom he'd appointed as judges in spite of their corruption and incompetence.

The people of Israel were sick of being ruled by amateurs. Now that they were a real nation, they wanted to be ruled by a professional king, just like everyone else.

Samuel gave in to their demands and agreed to find the people of Israel a king. Unfortunately,

Samuel conducted his talent search for a king in much the same way that one would put together a boy band. Samuel came across a handsome teenager named Saul, who was out looking for some lost donkeys. Thinking this was some sort of sign, Samuel made Saul king.

It turns out that donkey-catching is not the best qualification for being a head of state, and Saul was something of a disaster.

It wasn't long before the Philistines attacked again. In what has to be one of the most brilliant military maneuvers in ancient history, the Philistines began raiding Israel for the sole purpose of killing blacksmiths. After losing a few blacksmiths here, a few blacksmiths there, pretty soon hardly anyone was left who knew how to make weapons. Israel's soldiers now went screaming into battle armed with plows, head-shears, and wheelbarrows. Despite the fact that the army was fighting with agricultural implements, Israel still managed to win battles, thanks mostly to divine intervention.

Samuel realized he'd made a mistake. Saul was becoming increasingly paranoid and weird. He was breaking his deals with

God and, what's worse, stealing God's sheep.

God told Samuel to find his people another king. So Samuel went out looking for another talented young man to become king of Israel. The next guy to join Menudo was a twelve-year-old named David, whom Samuel discovered while the young man was watching his sheep and jamming on his harp.

"Here's the deal," Samuel explained. "God is going to ask things of you. Sometimes he'll ask you to show mercy. Sometimes he'll ask you to kill. God doesn't care if you are sweet or good. He only cares that you are his. God is going to make you King of Israel someday and all he asks in exchange is that you do what he asks of you."

Knowing that he'd lost God's confidence made Saul even more moody and unpredictable. The palace hired a harpist in hopes of soothing his nerves. And for a while, his relaxing new age compositions seemed to do the trick. In the long run, however, this was the worst thing they could have done for Saul's sanity, because the harpist they hired was David, the boy Samuel had appointed to replace Saul.

Saul's army was locked in a stalemate with the Philistines. They sent the new harp player out to the battlefield to take sandwiches and milk to the soldiers. While he was there, David saw this enormous Philistine, an eight foot-tall giant named Goliath, taunting the army of Israel, begging anyone who had the nerve to come down and fight him.

The torrent of abuse and obscenities got to David and he accepted the challenge. Amused, Goliath walked up to kill David as if he were going out to rake the leaves. The boy reacted impulsively by whipping out his slingshot and firing a racquetball-sized rock directly into Goliath's skull, killing him instantly. Then he lifted the giant's heavy sword into the air, and brought it down with a thud, decapitating Goliath.

The Philistines ran away, terrified by what the sandwich boy had just done to their best soldier.

Everybody loved David. He slew giants, won battles, and he was a terrific dancer. David's popularity left Saul feeling like an old calendar. When David asked to marry the princess, Michal, Saul tried to get rid of him by demanding the unhygienic dowry of two hundred Philistine foreskins. But this just added to his legend.

"Nobody told me he had a sling."

David killed two hundred Philistines, and cut off their foreskins, without even getting a rash.

Tired of subtlety, Saul simply sent a platoon of soldiers to go kill David in his sleep. But David's fast-thinking wife stuffed a mannequin into his bed to fool the assassins while David escaped, which is, quite literally, the oldest trick in the book.

Now on the lam, David went to the town of Nob, where some sympathetic priests gave him a few loaves of holy bread which was reserved for men who weren't sexually active. They also gave him Goliath's sword, which was being kept as a museum piece. When Saul heard about this, he was so peeved that he had everyone in the town of Nob put to death, including the priests.

Armed with Goliath's sword and his abstinence bread, David rallied together six hundred drinking buddies, whom he called his "Mighty Men." Saul and his army pursued David and the Mighty Men all over Israel. He was so hot on their trail that he almost stumbled upon them by accident at the Crag of Wild Goats. Saul walked into a cave to take a piss, unaware that David and his men were hiding inside.

The Mighty Men kept chuckling and nudging David, daring him to chop Saul's head off while he was peeing. Instead, David quietly cut off a small sliver of the king's robe. When Saul returned to his camp, David emerged from the cave and called out to him. The king turned to see David holding a piece of his robe, proving that he could have killed Saul if he'd wanted to.

This act of mercy filled Saul with shame, but not enough shame to stop him from his quest to kill David. Unable to live safely in Israel, David and his friends went to live with the Philistines. They spent their days drinking and robbing nearby towns. Whenever the king of the Philistines asked David to go raiding for them, he would. Only instead of attacking a town in Israel, he'd attack a Philistine town. He'd kill every man, woman and child, so no one could tattle on him. The king got his plunder and David got to kill Philistines. It was a win-win situation.

"I guess this is my life now," David said, resigning himself to being an armed burglar. But then, one day after coming back from work, David found the Philistines celebrating. They had just won a huge battle against Israel. Saul had committed suicide to avoid capture. True to his word, God had cleared the way to make David the new king of Israel.

A deal is a deal.

THE 2ᴺᴰ BOOK OF SAMUEL

 FTER A BIT OF persuading, most of which consisted of stabbing people in the gut, David was named King of Israel. David realized that there was more to becoming king than stabbing people in the gut, though. You're never really king until people think of you as king. But ruling your kingdom from a goat farm doesn't convince people you're a king. That's what conspicuous consumption is for. David realized that he needed a capital city, a palace, and a harem. The hallmarks of a legitimate ruler.

There was a city named Jebus on the border of Israel, which would make a perfectly nice capital city. So as his first official act in office, David conquered the city and killed off the locals. After mopping up all the blood and burning the corpses, David named his new capital Jerusalem, which means "City of Peace."

Then David built himself a palace. Once he felt cozy in his new throne, David ordered the Ark of the Covenant to be brought to Jerusalem, where it would be welcomed with a big parade. Samuel had long since died, but luckily, the prophet Nathan was on hand to arrange the rituals and make sure that the parade went off okay and the Ark didn't kill anybody.

Now, there are basically two kinds of people in the world: those who hate parades and morons. On this particular day, David was one of the latter. He was so excited by the parade that he stood up inside the royal box and started dancing. As the crowd cheered, his dancing got wilder and wilder. He threw his legs into the air. He flailed around so hard that he accidentally flashed his dick to the nation, which really upset his wife Michal.

"Nice, David, really nice," Michal said, scolding him. "It's bad enough that you did that God-awful dance, but then to expose yourself? To the slaves and everyone?"

David mumbled defensively.

"What did you say?" Michal growled.

"I said it was just a tip slip."

"It was a humiliation, is what it was! What, were you raised by farm animals?"

"Sort of."

David did not like being reminded of his redneck past. He went to bed without even giving Michal a goodnight kiss. Apparently God took David's side, because he cursed Michal with infertility, which may or may not be a nice way of saying that David stopped sleeping with her.

Though he had soured on Michal, David was still hot into women. He soon began collecting wives and concubines like they were Matchbox cars.

When David heard that the king of the neighboring Ammonites had died, David sent ambassadors to extend his condolences, one king to another. But the new king suspected David's ambassadors to be spies, so he thought it would be funny to square off the ends of their beards and cut their robes so short that they

"I'll see you in divorce court."

barely covered their testicles. Then he forced them to walk all the way back to Israel in this hilarious get-up.

"They don't respect me, do they?" David asked. The ambassadors in their mini-skirts shook their heads. "They don't think of me as a real king. So I have to respond the way a real king would." While the ambassadors changed their clothes, David declared war.

Needing to take a break from planning the war, David walked out onto his balcony, where he saw a woman named Bathsheba bathing outside his palace. He immediately became infatuated with her. When he found out that she was married, he sent her husband, a soldier named Uriah, on a suicide mission against the Ammonites. Once Uriah was out of the way, David married Bathsheba and she soon became his favorite wife.

David was an able general and a successful king. He routed the Ammonites and destroyed the Philistines. He had single-handedly taken Israel from a failed state to a world power. But his home life was a mess. His wives were constantly scheming against each other and their kids were at each other's throats.

Most of the real trouble started when his daughter Tamar was raped by her half-brother, Amnon. The law was unclear on this matter. On the one hand, having raped Tamar, the law now required Amnon to marry her. On the other hand, the law forbade brothers and sisters from marrying. It was a loophole Moses had failed to foresee.

David's solution to the dilemma was to forget the whole thing happened. So Tamar's older brother, Absalom, took justice into his own hands and killed her rapist.

Absalom, who was mostly known for his long, luxuriant hair, went on the run. Just as his father had done decades before, he gathered his friends and supporters and declared himself king. Then he rode into Jerusalem, stabbing anyone who disagreed. Not wanting to get stabbed, David left town and hid in the countryside. While David was raising an army to take back his throne, Absalom made himself at home in his father's palace.

Just like his father, Absalom wondered what he could do to convince people that he was the real king. The answer he came up with was to have sex with David's concubines on the roof, so that everyone could see him.

Leading an army, with the throne of Israel on the line, David returned in force, and creamed Absalom's army. While fleeing the battle, Absalom got his long, beautiful hair caught on a tree branch which pulled him off his horse and left him dangling helplessly from a tree. When his pursuers found him hanging there like a piñata, they couldn't help but whack at him with their swords and spears. Unfortunately, no candy came pouring out of Absalom, just blood and organs.

Despite the fact that he had stolen his throne and had sex with his girlfriends, David was torn by grief when he heard that Absalom was dead.

David's reign was a big success, but he was losing sons and daughters left and right. The palace, the capital city, all his war trophies, they did nothing for him now. He was a heartbroken and haunted man.

"Haven't I done everything God has asked of me?" David wondered. "Didn't I kill all the right foreigners? Why would God do this to me?"

The Prophet Nathan had an answer to this riddle. He told David about a rich farmer who lived nearby. This farmer was so rich he was practically shitting sheep and goats. His neighbor, on the other hand, was a poor man who had only one sheep and that little animal was all he owned in the world. The rich farmer had him killed and added the dead man's sheep to his flock of thousands.

"Your majesty, what do you think we should do with this farmer?" he asked.

King David responded immediately, "What do you mean? Bring him here. I'll kill him right now."

Nathan then revealed that David was the farmer. The farmer's crime was what he himself had done to poor Uriah. "If you would have a man executed for doing what you have done, then how can you expect any less from God? God might want you to be king. But just because God put you in a position to pull shit like that," Nathan said, "that doesn't mean he has to let you get away with it."

THE 1ST BOOK OF KINGS

ING DAVID HAD gotten old. He was so cold and frail that the court appointed a young woman to snuggle with him in his bed. No, they didn't have sex. Though the court did make a point of hiring someone beautiful, just to put a little sizzle in his chicken.

The presence of a human hot water bottle notwithstanding, David was dying. His wife Bathsheba was afraid that once he died, her son Solomon would be killed by his older brothers.

So Bathsheba tricked David into passing over the crown prince Adonijah and naming Solomon as his successor, even though Solomon was his youngest son. In what would later become a common tactic in scams against the elderly, she told David that he had already promised to do it, but had simply forgotten.

David died, making Solomon King of Israel. When Adonijah stopped by the palace for a rather awkward family visit, Bathsheba met him at the door.

"What do you want?" she asked.

"Look, I just wanted to say that you have nothing to worry about from me. Solomon's king now and I'm totally cool with that," he said. "Things don't always work out the way they should—I've come to accept that. Anyway, I'm not here to cause you any trouble. All I want to ask from you is one tiny favor."

"Like what?"

"I want to marry the human hot water bottle."

"Really? That's it? I thought you were going to ask for half the kingdom or something."

"I guess I'm just a hopeless romantic!" he shrugged.

Bathsheba went to Solomon and told him about Adonijah's request.

"A pretty reasonable request under the circumstances," she added.

"Woman, please! If I approve this marriage, I might as well have my brother fitted for the crown. My claim to the throne is shaky at best. Suppose they get married and the human hot water bottle then concocts a story about how you or I poisoned dad? Or that we smothered him in his sleep? How would that look for us?

Plus, she has friends like all over the palace. Who's to say one of them wouldn't slip a little arsenic in my soup in exchange for being promoted to 'Taster of Meats?' Geez, I can't believe you fell for that. Way to go, MOM!"

Solomon now knew that his brother was planning a coup d'état and he reacted to the crisis with all the subtlety and aplomb of his father, which is to say, he paid a guy to club Adonijah in the skull. Solomon then went on a spree, clubbing in the heads of Saul's relatives and David's old generals. This royal game of whack-a-mole didn't end until Solomon felt that he had removed everyone who was a threat to his rule.

Establishing himself as king was a bloody process, just as it was for his father, but eventually he prevailed. God, who always likes a winner, granted Solomon one wish. Great power, enormous wealth, a ten-inch dong, all the normal wish stuff. Instead of choosing any of those, Solomon asked God to grant him great wisdom. God was so thrilled to get such a noble wish that he made Solomon the wisest man in the world.

It wasn't long before Solomon's new smarts were put to the test.

For some reason, being King of Israel meant occasionally presiding over custody battles. Solomon was hearing a case between two prostitutes, each of whom was claiming to be the mother of this baby. Since it was just one prostitute's word against another, Solomon ruled that the only fair thing to do was to cut the baby down the middle and give each woman half.

"Fine with me," one of the women said. "Half a baby is better than none."

The other woman collapsed onto the floor and pleaded for Solomon to let the other prostitute keep the baby.

Having coaxed these radically different reactions from the women, Solomon figured that the one who was begging to save the child's life must be its true mother, so he let her keep the baby. In its entirety.

Word of his shrewd decision quickly spread throughout the land. As luck would have it, this story also worked as an allegory, a moral injunction against any upstarts or ambitious members of the royal family who, like the bad whore, would tear the country in half with civil war rather than let it live intact under Solomon, who may or may not be its rightful mother.

Under Solomon's wise and undisputed rule, Israel entered its golden age. The country doubled in size and Solomon became the richest man in the world. He ate figs and gazelle meat until his legs went silly. He gave lectures on fish and birds. People came from all over the world to be dazzled by his brilliance.

The time had come for Solomon to build God his temple. God had given Solomon a set of blueprints to work from, and Solomon put tens of thousands of people to work on the building. When it was finished, it was a world class temple. Its interior walls were tastefully lined with carved cedar, except for the room where the Ark was going to be kept, where the walls were lined with solid gold. A little flashy, but that's the way God liked things. The Temple was decorated with bronze bulls and furnished with hundreds of washing bowls and wick-trimmers. God couldn't have been happier.

"Let's do this thing."

Once he finished the Temple, Solomon celebrated by building himself a massive new palace. He needed one. Like his father, Solomon had a taste for the ladies and soon had over 700 wives. Solomon was now free to spend the rest of his days hanging out with his wives, composing proverbs, and trying to get his music career off the ground.

The good times didn't last forever, though. God was jealous because in addition to his temple, Solomon had also built temples to all his foreign wives' gods.

"Why would he do that?" God wondered. "Didn't I grant him a wish? He even built temples for Moloch and Chemosh and those guys are TOTAL dicks! You know what? I'm done with Solomon. And Israel. The next time they get into trouble, they can ask their girlfriend Moloch to save them."

After a nice long reign, Solomon died, and the whole country immediately started a long slide into the ditch. Israel became embroiled in civil war, and unlike the baby with the prostitutes, the kingdom actually was cut in half, with the new guy becoming King of Israel in the north and Solomon's son taking control of the new Kingdom of Judah in the south.

The once great kingdom was now two mediocre ones, ruled by a succession of weak and corrupt men.

The worst of the lot was a guy named Ahab, who reigned as King of Israel. His wife, Jezebel, was a pagan who killed prophets as a sort of pastime. Ahab and Jezebel worshiped a rain god named Baal.

This made God so angry that he sent the prophet Elijah to challenge Baal to a cook-off. The priests of Baal and Elijah each set up altars. They each killed an ox and prayed to their respective gods to send fire down from heaven to cook the sacrificial meat. The statue of Baal, sat there dumbly, looking straight ahead while his priests danced and flailed themselves before him.

God fared much better. As if from a divine propane tank, a searing jet of flame shot down from heaven, instantly barbecuing the meat and incinerating Baal's priests. God had won the cook-off. And as was common in these ancient game shows, the losers were killed on the spot. But the royal family remained unmoved, shrugging it off as "one of those things," and carrying on with their pagan lives.

Ahab came across a piece of land that he thought would make an absolutely perfect place for his vegetable garden. He went to the landowner and offered to buy it. The man graciously turned down the offer, explaining that the land had been in his family for generations.

Later, at dinner, Ahab told Jezebel about his failed land deal.

"It's really too bad. It would have been perfect. There was a nice patch for cucumbers, I could have planted rhubarb in the corner... a real shame it didn't work out."

"Oh, you big pussy," said Jezebel, who was always taunting Ahab, "is that how a king acts? Don't worry, I'll get you your vegetable garden, Sally."

Jezebel invited the landowner to dinner at the palace. When he arrived, she seated him between a couple of dubious characters. In the middle of the dinner, one of the men stood up and accused the landowner of cursing the king, just as Jezebel had paid him to. "I heard it, too!" the other man said, corroborating the charge.

Jezebel called in the guards and had the poor, sputtering landowner killed on the spot for treason. His land now belonged to the king.

Ahab was happily planning his new vegetable garden when Elijah showed up at the gate and confronted him.

"I came here to tell you that God will not tolerate a vegetable garden built on the blood of an innocent man," Elijah said. "God is through with you and your rotten wife. As punishment for your crimes, your dynasty will be destroyed, your family devoured by birds and dogs. Have fun with your peas."

Not long after, Ahab got shot with an arrow during a battle and died. They buried his body before any animals got to it, but dogs did get in to lick up his blood, so Elijah gets partial credit on that one.

THE 2ᴺᴰ BOOK OF KINGS

 OMEWHERE ALONG the line, God and the Jews became more than just friends. In fact, God considered himself to be married to the Jews. Like most marriages, it was primarily a non-sexual affair, but unlike most marriages, it was anything but snoozy. God's marriage to the Jews was a tempestuous, rancorous affair. The Jews were always drinking too much and flirting with other gods, while God would lose his temper and storm out of the house.

Every now and then, God would appoint a prophet to act as a sort of marriage counselor. These prophets were always trying to patch things up between God and the Jews.

The Prophet Elijah's marriage counseling career had come to an end. For his retirement party, God sent a golden chariot, which came swooping down from the sky and carried Elijah naked up to Heaven. Elijah's marriage counseling practice passed on to his protégé, Elisha.

"Let that be a lesson to you."

Elisha cursed the idolaters who'd forged the emotional wedge between God and his people, and he validated God's feelings of neglect. Elisha then tried to take the Jews on an "empathy adventure," getting them to understand God's feelings of abandonment. To help him with his work, God granted Elisha miraculous powers. Elisha traveled the country, using his powers to remind the Jews of the spark they once felt for God.

Most of the miracles Elisha performed were quite practical and helpful. He focused on things like multiplying small amounts of food into great feasts, making water appear in the desert, or healing people of food poisoning. He even helped a man retrieve a lost axe head from a river.

"Wow, thanks, Elisha!" people would say. "Maybe we can work things out with God, after all."

Not all of his miracles were so benign, though. Elisha was bald and touchy about it. A lot of bald men are. When he arrived at the town of Bethel, he was teased by a group of boys who called him "baldy." Elisha responded to their taunts by summoning a team of wild she-bears. The bears mauled the boys to death, leaving the bloody remains of forty-two children littered on the ground.

Nobody knows why Elisha didn't just summon a full head of hair.

Ahab was dead, but his Baal-worshiping family still ruled Israel. Elisha felt that a change in leadership would make it easier for Israel and God to rediscover their lost intimacy and rekindle the embers of mutual trust. So Elisha talked a local thug named Jehu into taking over the government.

Jehu rode to the home of the new king of Israel, Joram. When Joram saw Jehu in the distance, he and his entourage hopped in a chariot and drove out to meet him.

"What are you doing here?" Joram asked.

"Well, if you must know," Jehu replied, "I'm here to kill you."

When Joram tried to race away in his chariot, Jehu shot him in the back with an arrow. Joram slumped over, dead. Panicked, his friends dumped Joram's body into a nearby field and fled the scene. Ironically, the field where the corpse of Joram lay, being devoured by birds, was the same field Ahab had stolen to make his illicit vegetable garden.

When Jehu arrived at the royal palace, Jezebel finished putting on her makeup and slowly walked out to the balcony, flanked by her eunuch bodyguards. "Oh look, it's that hillbilly who killed my grandson," she said. "What do you have to say for yourself?"

"Just that there are job openings in my new kingdom."

Knowing a good career move when they saw it, the eunuchs threw Jezebel off the balcony to her death. Her body was dragged off and eaten by dogs. Somewhere God high-fived Elijah, who had scored 2.5 out of 3 on his prophecy.

As the new King of Israel, Jehu asked the priests of Baal to meet him at their temple, so he could get off on the right foot with their god. This turned out to be a sting operation. When they showed up, Jehu killed all the priests. Then he converted Baal's temple into a public restroom. As a joke, Jehu changed the sign on the doorway from Beelzebul, which meant "Baal: Lord of the Heavens" to Beelzebub, which meant "Baal: Lord of Flies."

Elisha was right about the positive impact regime change would have on God's relationship with the Jews. With Jehu in charge, God and Israel were able to begin the healing process and it saved their marriage, at least for a while.

Elisha's career as a marriage counselor had also come to an end, by which, I mean he died. No chariot ride for Elisha, though, he was interred at a local cemetery. As an interesting side note, another funeral was going on at a nearby grave when it was interrupted by a bandit attack. The terrified pall-bearers ditched their dead loved one into Elisha's grave by mistake. When the dead man toppled down onto Elisha's still miraculous corpse, he instantly came back to life. I can only imagine how confused he must have been.

After King Jehu died, Israel's kings went right back to worshiping foreign gods, and God's relationship with Israel took a turn for the worse. God was constantly threatening to leave. Eventually, God would make good on his threats. Having finally had enough, God let the Assyrians conquer Israel and evict the population, forever scattering ten of the twelve tribes of Israel.

Judah, Israel's cousin to the south, was so disturbed by Israel's demise that the King of Judah immediately called for his nation to recommit itself to God.

There is perhaps no surer sign that a marriage is in serious trouble than when a couple decides to renew their vows. The king of Judah paid for a big, glitzy ceremony at the temple to reaffirm Judah's dedication to God. It was a beautiful ceremony and everyone agreed that God looked great. But somehow, the whole ritual stunk of forced smiles and masked contempt.

People congratulated and toasted the couple, but as they sipped their sparkling wine and ate their hors d'oeuvres, they secretly chuckled to each other about how it would never last.

THE 1ˢᵀ BOOK OF CHRONICLES

WHEN **DAVID WAS** King of Israel, God wasn't having to constantly bail Israel out the way he did in the old days. So God refocused his considerable free time and energy on his new hobby: scrapbooking.

He put the priests to work compiling thousands of tidbits for his Precious Memories scrapbook. They gathered enough of these to fill the first nine chapters of Chronicles with birth records, genealogies, and gossipy details on hundreds of people going all the way back to Adam and Eve. The priests tirelessly assembled volume after volume of sentimental keepsakes.

God decided that he needed a house of his own, someplace where he could relax, keep in touch with friends, and work on his scrapbooks. A place where the priests could be kept stocked with parchment, glue and clip art.

David had come a long way since his days of guarding sheep and playing harp for tips at the palace. He was not only king, but God's best friend to boot. God and David were inseparable. Once he became king, David hired some movers to bring the Ark of the Covenant to his palace so he and God could be roommates. David imagined all the trouble two guys at the top of their game to get into.

"People will probably give us matching nicknames, like 'Thunder and Crash,'" he thought. "They'll say, 'There they go, Thunder & Crash.' We'll totally run the place."

God was riding the Ark into Jerusalem, sitting on his Mercy Seat, when the road suddenly started getting bumpy. The Ark began slipping around on the ox cart. One of the movers reached up to keep the Ark from falling off, but when he touched it, God immediately struck the man dead. God doesn't like people touching the Ark.

When he heard about this, David wondered if God might not be such a great roommate, after all. So instead of moving the Ark into the palace, he stashed it in a tent where the priests could help God with his scrapbooking, and sacrifice tasty treats to him, but hopefully he wouldn't kill anyone.

David put together a big parade to celebrate the arrival of the Ark. There was music, burnt offerings, and free cake for everyone. Then he showed God to his tent.

"I thought I was going to live with you," God said.

"Oh, you wouldn't like that," David replied, "I snore, and I'm always walking around the palace naked. Trust me, you'll be much happier in your own place."

But God was not happy. God hated camping. He wanted a palace of his own like David's. So he told David that he should have his son Solomon build him a nice, spacious temple.

"Then I can get down to some *serious* scrapbooking!" God told himself.

Meanwhile, David spent most of his time away from home fighting wars. In the middle of all his fighting, David decided to take a census, which really ticked God off for some reason.

"Maybe this is a chance to show David who's really in charge," God wondered.

To teach him a lesson, God gave David a choice of three punishments: either Israel could suffer three years of famine,

"I have an order for Ark D. Covenant?"

three months of losing battles, or three days of God's bare-knuckled, no-holds-barred wrath.

Hoping to get the punishment over with as soon as possible, David chose the three days of divine wrath. In just 72 hours, God managed to wipe out seventy thousand people. David was so distraught that he ripped his clothes and poured ash on himself and begged God to stop.

"Fine, quit your blubbering, you big baby," God said. "I've got parchment which needs gluing, anyway."

God threw himself back into a new Creative Memories scrapbook. At this point, First Chronicles takes a break to list six chapters worth of notable people and birth records, including those of God's favorite musicians and soldiers. It even gives a shout-out to some of Jerusalem's gatekeepers.

His wars over, his kingdom secure, David decided to spend more time at home, hanging out with the family. He rediscovered his love of music and once again took up jamming on his harp, writing songs. His son, Solomon, turned out to be musically inclined as well.

Before he died, David gathered all the timber, gold and jewelry he'd accumulated as spoils of war over the years and gave them to Solomon along with the architectural blueprints for God's new temple.

"Whatever you do," David advised his son, "don't drag your feet on building this temple. God will get sick of scrapbooking before long. Everyone does. When that happens, trust me, he'll be looking for reasons to be pissed off."

"Touch it. I dare you."

THE 2ND BOOK OF CHRONICLES

FTER SOLOMON WAS crowned king, he eagerly began construction on the temple.

Like most rich nations, Israel was completely dependent on foreign labor. Solomon knew that in order to bring a really big construction project in under budget, you needed illegal aliens, and plenty of them. So Solomon rounded up all the immigrants in Israel and put them to work cutting stones in the quarry and carrying them to the construction site. Then he hired the best architects, artisans and interior decorators from all over the world to put the Temple together and imbue it with an opulent, yet dignified, sense of elegance.

When completed, the Temple was tricked out with gold plating, bas reliefs of palm trees and jewel-studded walls. It even came with apples hanging from chains, like charms from a necklace. It had dozens of hand-washing stations for the priests, an enormous altar, and crowns and water basins, all made out of the best gold.

For the grand opening party, Solomon slaughtered twenty thousand oxen and sheep. God was so impressed by his new house that he sent fire down from heaven, convection baking all that meat for everyone who'd come to marvel at the Temple.

Riding atop the Ark, God was ceremoniously moved into his new house. Nobody had ever seen anything quite like it. It was a true architectural marvel, and it soon became famous all over the world as the Temple of Solomon.

During the housewarming party, one of the priests had made the egregious error of looking inside the Ark, but God was so mellowed out by the good time he was having that he didn't even kill the guy.

Later, that priest told his story to the others, who were positively dumbstruck.

"You looked INSIDE the Ark?" one asked. "That's insane!"

"What was inside?" Another asked.

"It was empty," the priest shrugged, "except for a couple of stone tablets."

All this time, the only thing God kept in the Ark were the tablets he had given to Moses centuries before. The deal he had made with the Jews to be his people.

"You've done an amazing job on the Temple," God told Solomon. "It's just as I imagined it would be, and I love it. This is probably the happiest day of my life!

"Solomon, can I tell you something?" God said, taking Solomon aside for a moment. "I just wanted to say that I know I can seem a little petty sometimes, demanding solid gold handsinks and apples hanging from the ceiling.

"And I know I can be a bit of a hothead. But there's a reason why I get so jealous. The truth is that I love these people, but sometimes I feel like they don't love me back. And that drives me *crazy*. The reason the Temple means so much to me is that I want it to be a place my people are proud of. I want them to be proud of *me*.

"As much as I love my new temple, I would rather tear it down than see it become another museum to a forgotten god nobody takes seriously anymore. Solomon, I've never told anyone this before, but I don't know what I'd do if the Jews ever stopped loving me."

The next morning, as people sobered up from the grand

opening party, everyone was truly taken aback at how wonderful God's temple was. Overnight, the Temple of Solomon became the beating heart of Israel.

Unfortunately, nothing lasts forever. After the initial excitement over the Temple had died down, people gradually turned away from God and began once again worshiping foreign gods. The kings who followed began building temples to other gods, and everyone seemed to agree that they were now too rich and sophisticated to be expected to honor the deal their ancestors had made with God back when they were a homeless nation of hikers.

God watched as he and his temple were gradually reduced to little more than a tourist trap.

God was so heartbroken that after a while he couldn't even be bothered to get out of bed, not for miracles, not for scrapbooking, not even to save his people from foreign invasion.

God barely even noticed as his people were conquered, first by Assyrians and then Babylonians. When the Babylonians showed up at the Temple, they knocked down its walls, stole its treasure, and set the whole place on fire. The priests were forced to pick out the Ark and all of God's scrapbooks out of the burned ruins. The temple treasure, the priests, the Ark, God's scrapbooks, and anyone who was anyone were carted off to Babylon as trophies while Jerusalem burned to the ground, leaving only the smoldering ashes of a dead nation.

"I suppose now we have to read his blog too."

EZRA

AFTER CONQUERING Judah, the Babylonians annihilated Jerusalem, tearing down the city walls, razing the Temple, stealing its treasure and forcing all its brightest, prettiest, and richest people to move to Babylon. The Jews lived in exile for fifty years before Babylon was itself gobbled up by the Persian Empire.

The Persian king, Cyrus, didn't see any reason why people should be forced to live in Babylon against their will, so he let the Jews return to their homeland. In fact, he picked up the bill for their return trip. What a nice young man!

Despite this perk, hardly anyone wanted to return to the Promised Land. The whole place was in ruins, there were weeds everywhere, and they had all become accustomed to the good life in Babylon.

Cyrus thought he could lure them back to their homeland if he rebuilt the Temple. So he sent a party of Jews back to Jerusalem to rebuild it.

"The good news is, I found God. The bad news is, you're no longer good enough for me."

This didn't make the neighboring kingdoms very happy. The last thing they wanted was an exciting new tourist attraction in the next country over. In order to keep the Temple from being rebuilt, they turned to the most devastating tactic known to the ancient world: the letter-writing campaign:

Dear King of Persia, Master of a Hundred Nations,

Greetings from the Trans-Euphrates! First off, we just wanted to say how much we LOVE the Persian Empire. These are exciting times, and we look forward to many years of rewarding subjugation. Unfortunately, not everyone seems to be as on board with Persian rule as we are. We recently heard that the Jews (and jeez, I really hate to be a snitch!) are rebuilding the walls to their city. Do you know if they're allowed to do that? I thought they were just supposed to be rebuilding their temple. It seems odd that they would be rebuilding their city walls instead. Unless, of course, they were planning some sort of revolt. Just saying. Hey, maybe that's something you want to look into!

Signed,
Your loyal subjects and biggest fans

When the king got the letter, he called a halt to all construction until the building inspector could look into it. After years of delay, when it became clear that the Jews weren't planning a revolt, work on the Temple was allowed to resume, which prompted yet another letter.

Dearest Ruler of Heaven and Earth, Lord of the Ants and the Birds and All That,

Hello again from the Trans-Euphrates! Hey, I just wanted to give you a heads up: we were driving through Judah last weekend, and couldn't help but notice that the Jews are back at work on their temple. When we asked to see their building permit, they didn't have one, but said that one was on file back in Persia. Is that true? Hate to be a stickler, but maybe they should stop work on the temple until the permit can be verified?

Signed,
Concerned citizens

Work on the Temple was delayed once again while the king retrieved the correct permits from the archives. Sick of being bothered by these people, the king sent them a response:

Dear Friends in the Trans-Euphrates,

After a long, exhaustive search, we have located the permit you requested and found it to be in working order. I'm saddened that the legality of this temple's construction is causing you so many sleepless nights. I really don't want this matter to weigh on your minds anymore, so from here on out, work on the temple will continue unabated, and if anyone sends me another letter or tries to stop the construction in any way, I will pull a beam out of their house and impale them on it.

Hopefully this will finally put your concerns to rest.

Signed,
Your Loving Monarch

Work on the Temple continued undisturbed. The King of Persia then sent a letter to one of his Jewish scribes, named Ezra.

Dear Ezra,

Persia recognizes that a valued and motivated workforce is the key to a successful empire. That is why we are committed to celebrating our subjects' unique cultures and religious beliefs.

Unfortunately, we seem to be experiencing some challenges in convincing your people to reclaim their rich and vibrant way of life. Here in the Persian Empire, we believe that citizenship begins with education and ends with empowerment. To that end, we would like you to lead a coterie of priests, judges, and artists back to Jerusalem to rediscover old traditions, foster your religious identity, and promote your ancestral homeland as a beacon of inclusion and opportunity within the Persian Empire.

To help you get started, please accept the enclosed four tons of silver, eighteen tons of wheat, and six hundred gallons of wine.

In Commitment to Excellence Through Diversity and Empowerment, The King of Persia

Excited to see the land he'd grown up hearing so much about, Ezra eagerly took the king up on his offer.

Now, as any seasoned traveler will tell you, when you romanticize a place in your mind, you're bound to be disappointed when you get there. And this is what happened to Ezra. When he finally got back to Jerusalem, he was shocked. The place was a wreck. The Jews who were still living there had gotten incredibly sloppy in their religious observances and nothing seemed to be done by the book. And worst of all, the men had all taken to marrying pagans. This drove Ezra nuts, a point he made clear by pulling his beard out with his bare hands.

"Have you people learned nothing?" He screamed, chin still hurting from the recent beard-pull. "The whole reason God allowed us to be conquered in the first place was because we started worshiping foreign gods. And the reason we started worshiping foreign gods was because we started messing around with foreign women. Now, here we are, given a second chance after fifty years in exile, and what are you doing? You're starting the cycle all over again!"

"Okay, okay, you're right," the men shouted back. "We've sinned. We married foreign women, and got a little kinky with their gods. But the damage is done. We have *kids* with these women now. What do you want us to do about it?"

"There's only one thing to do," Ezra replied. "You have to send them away. Your pagan wives, your little pagan kids. It's a shitty thing to do, I know, but it's your own fault for disobeying the law in the first place."

"What? Send them away? Now?

It's raining! They can't go out on a night like this. Besides, these are our families we're talking about. We need time to say good-bye."

"Yeah!" someone else shouted, "Ever hear of closure?"

Ezra reluctantly agreed. "All right, you can wait until the good weather returns. But then you've got to get rid of them."

The day came when the skies cleared and the sun came out. All the men who'd married foreign women lined their families up, gave them sack lunches, and tearfully sent them on the road to God knows where.

"I'm not a hard man," Ezra explained, "but it's my job to rebuild our people, to recreate our way of life. If I had done nothing, our blood, our customs, our religion would have been compromised and watered down until we were just another group of freeballing shepherds.

"Sometimes diversity means getting rid of people who aren't like you."

NEHEMIAH

EHEMIAH LIVED A comfortable life in Persia. He was King Artaxerxes' cup-bearer. Whenever the king got peckish, Nehemiah would bring him a tray of roast quail tongues or hand-slain gazelle. When the king asked for wine, Nehemiah would bring him a woody red or a buttery white. And whenever the king was having a bad day, Nehemiah would crack jokes or say something validating about his hair. The two men were as close as lips and teeth.

Nehemiah was Jewish, and was excited to return to his people's homeland, even though he'd been born and raised in Babylon. Nehemiah asked the king if he could take some vacation time to go help rebuild Jerusalem's walls. He was such a cool boss, that the king not only let Nehemiah go, but put him in charge of the city.

Nehemiah used this adventure to take a crack at writing his memoirs:

> You Can go Home Again
> by Nehemiah

It felt good to be back home. Even though 'home' was someplace I'd never been before.

One day I was picking out table settings, the next I was running a city. Having been a servant all my life, it felt awkward to suddenly be The Man. Speaking metaphorically, of course. As a eunuch, I have no dick or balls worth speaking of.

First, let me explain something to you: a city is basically a species of animal. A city without walls is like a turtle without a shell. A city without watchtowers is like a cat without eyes. A city without a gate is like a cow without a mouth.

We built walls, we built watchtowers. Needing a mouth, we built the Fish Gate, so the food could flow in. Needing an ass, we built the Dung Gate, so the shit could flow out. Rebuilding a city is like resurrecting a dead animal. You not only need to bring it back to life, you have to keep the wolves and coyotes away while you do it.

When the neighboring countries noticed we were rebuilding the city walls, they laughed us off. But as the wall grew taller, the laughter was replaced by threats. Every week, new messages would arrive, threatening war if we continued working on the walls.

Stopping work on the wall was out of the question. We all agreed that we had come too far to quit, whatever the cost. And yet, I knew these were not idle threats. So I had to take half my work force off the wall, arm them, and use them as guards. With only half the work-force building the wall, this meant everyone had to work double shifts. Despite their heroism and sacrifice, I knew my builders couldn't carry on much longer like that.

Things got worse. I learned that many of my workers, who had literally poured their blood and sweat into that wall, were forced to mortgage their homes and go into debt, just so they could afford to work on the wall. So when I heard that our own merchants and noblemen were taking advantage, raising interest rates and foreclosing on homes, I totally lost my shit.

These were heroes, building the wall and guarding the city from attack, protecting these greedy assholes who were then charging them for the privilege. I gathered all the lenders together in a room and I told these guys that if they wanted to live in our city when the wall was finished, then all this subprime mortgage shit would have to stop, NOW. What's the point of guarding against a foreign invasion when you're being enslaved from within?

Although the invasion never came, the foreign kings still tried to stop me from completing the wall. They sent me a letter vaguely accusing me of walling off the city so I could become king and lead a revolt against Persia. They summoned me to a series of hearings to discuss the matter. I saw no point in trying to talk them out of believing rumors they themselves had made up. I had too much work to do, anyway, so I ignored them.

Soon afterward, a man came running up and said there was a group of armed men coming to kill me. He pleaded with me to hide in the Temple. "Hurry, run to the Temple! There's a gang of mercenaries right outside the city! Quick, hide in the Temple! Seriously, they're coming! Oh my God, they're huge! They've got swords and these huge axe things and everything!"

I wasn't sure why he was so eager to see me hide in the Temple, but something about the situation just didn't smell right, so I simply kept working. Later on, I figured out what he was trying to do. The neighboring kings had learned about an obscure Jewish law that eunuchs aren't allowed in the Temple. If they could trick me into going inside, they thought I would be stoned to death or something.

*"I may be a eunuch, but I've got balls
enough to kick your ass."*

After two months of danger, sleep deprivation, and hard work, the walls of Jerusalem had been rebuilt. And all because I followed one simple maxim: when in doubt, keep working.

It might seem a little trite, all this trouble over a stupid wall. But you've got to understand, it was the wall that finally allowed people to return to Jerusalem without having to worry about being overrun by thieves, marauders, and rapists. A few hardscrabble pioneers can make a go of it in a lawless wasteland, but if you want the artists, priests, and scribes to come, then you need a wall to protect them. And those are the people who create your culture, write your history. It might be construction workers who build your nation, and soldiers who guard it, but it's the nerds who make it a civilization.

To celebrate the completion of the wall, we threw a giant celebration. There were musicians playing on top of the wall. There were choirs at the Fish Gate, singing out of the mouth of the city. There were choirs at the Dung Gate, singing out the ass of the city. You could hear us for miles around. Then, Ezra emerged from the Temple and stood at the altar. A hush fell across the entire city as he began to read from the Torah.

As I looked around, I could see tears rolling down the cheeks of the old people and it occurred to me: it had been fifty years since these people had heard these words read aloud in public. It had been fifty years since we were all gathered together in one place. Soon tears were staining the faces of every man and woman in the city. Most of us didn't even grow up here, but it didn't matter. We all felt, perhaps for the first time ever, that we were home.

ESTHER

 HEN XERXES WAS King of Persia, he once threw an epic party that lasted a whole six months. At one point during the party, the king got drunk and ordered his wife Vashti to dance in front of his friends to show off her tight young body.

"Yeah, I don't think that's going to happen," Vashti said.

"Whatever," King Xerxes shrugged. "Let's do some Jello shots…"

His advisors took Vashti's refusal much more seriously, though. They told Xerxes that if he let Vashti off the hook, women all over the empire would start disobeying their husbands, sparking a wildfire of feminist bedlam. Trying to put the genie back into the bottle, King Xerxes was forced to divorce Vashti. Now Xerxes needed a new queen, so he set up a worldwide beauty pageant. The winner was a young Jewish woman named Esther.

As part of her prize, Esther was given a year's worth of beauty products, fancy dining, and luxury accommodations at the king's palace. One of the king's advisors was a Jewish man named Mordecai, who happened to be Esther's uncle. Mordecai told her not to mention her family, as that would reveal that she was Jewish, which he felt might somehow queer the deal.

"He might not like ethnics," he warned her.

Soon after Esther and Xerxes were married, Mordecai stumbled upon a plot by a couple of bitter old eunuchs to assassinate the king. Mordecai exposed the plotters and saved King Xerxes' life, a fact which was duly entered into public record with a gold star next to Mordecai's name.

In addition to his sexy new wife, the king also had a new prime minister, named Haman. To celebrate his promotion, the king allowed Haman to parade through town while everyone in the streets bowed and shouted wonderful things about him. Haman really got off on parades and ass-kissing and was having a mind-blowingly good time. But when he returned to the palace, the best day of his life abruptly turned to shit. Because there was one person out of the whole city who refused to bow as he walked past. The party-pooper was

"Furthermore, belly dancing is degrading, mysogynistic, and devalues the intellectual contribution of women."

Esther's uncle, Mordecai. Haman immediately complained to the king.

"Bowing's against my religion," Mordecai explained.

"It's a religious thing," the king said, closing the matter.

This slight continued to haunt Haman, however, stinging him in his sleep like a pillowcase full of scorpions. Haman vowed to have his revenge by not only murdering Mordecai, but his entire race as well.

"That'll teach them to ruin a parade."

So one day, while the king was buried under paperwork, Haman slipped a decree into the pile ordering the execution of Mordecai and all the Jews in the Persian Empire.

"What's this?" The king asked.

"Oh, nothing. Just a death warrant for some fringe group who have their own set of laws. Apparently, they don't think your laws are good enough."

"Well, we can't have a bunch of haters running loose. If you think it's a good idea, go ahead and put my seal on it," the king said, tossing his signet ring to Haman. It was a casual genocide.

Perhaps hoping to later turn the extermination of the Jews into a board game, Haman used a set of dice, or *purim*, to select the date on which the genocide would begin. It's from these dice that the Jews get the name for their "Feast of Purim."

Late one night, Xerxes was suffering from insomnia. He started reading the public records, hoping to bore himself to sleep. While reading, he saw the gold star next to Mordecai's name and realized that he'd forgotten to reward Mordecai for saving his life. So the next morning, he asked Haman what he should do to reward someone who'd done the king a really big favor. Haman, of course, thought the king was referring to him.

"Well, I think anybody would love a really nice parade. Not just any parade, though. They should be led through the city on your horse and wearing your favorite jacket. Oh! And someone should run in front of him shouting his praises and everyone should be forced to look at him and think he's cool. Now, THAT would be a parade!" Haman said, ticklish

with anticipation.

"Perfect!" The king replied. "Could you do it?"

"Do what?"

"Make the arrangements. You know, be the guy who leads him through town, shouting nice things about him, telling everyone he's my best friend in the world, that sort of thing? I want to give Mordecai a parade he'll never forget."

"Who?"

"Mordecai. You know Mordecai, don't you? That Jewish guy? He saved my life once and I totally forgot to thank him. Scatterbrained!" the king said, wobbling his crown around on his head.

Haman burned with humiliation. He returned from the degrading venture even more determined to have his revenge on Mordecai. To make his vengence even sweeter, Haman built a special, seventy-five foot tall spike on which to impale Mordecai.

When Mordecai found out about the king's decree, and the approaching date of the ordered extermination of the Jews, he went to Esther and begged her to say something to the king.

"I know what I said before, about keeping the Jew thing under wraps, but the next time you're having sex with him, it might not hurt to let it slip, you know, that *you're* Jewish. You know, it could help the rest of us out."

"Yeah, but I can't just tackle the king in the hallway and start humping his leg. I have to wait for him to call for me. If I show up unannounced, his guards will put me to death. And he hasn't called for me in, like, a month."

"Well, you'd better think of something. We can't let the future of our race be decided by whether or not the king gets horny in the next couple of weeks."

Esther was in a bind. Days passed, the date of the planned genocide approached and still the king had not called for her. Finally, she worked up the nerve and burst in on the king while he was working.

"Esther! Honeybee! What's the matter? You look nervous. Oh, is it that rule about being killed for coming to me unannounced? Oh, don't worry about that! That's just an old palace by-law. Tell me, how've you been? What's going on in your life?"

"Oh, cheetah lips, you're so good to me, and I hate to ask favors of you, but I do have something really important I need to ask you. I see that you're busy,

though, so I'll tell you what. Why don't you and Haman join me for dinner tomorrow. I'll cook up some antelope steaks, and I'll tell you all about it."

The next day, Esther laid out three place settings. After enjoying a pleasant, light-hearted dinner, the king turned to Esther and asked, "So what was that favor you wanted to ask me?"

"Oh, yeah. It's nothing, really. But it turns out that there's a law on the books that all the Jews are supposed to be killed. Well, I don't think I've ever mentioned it, but I'm Jewish. So, according to your law, I'm going to be killed, along with my family and all of my people."

"What? What are you talking about?" the king asked, stunned. "I never passed any law like that!"

"Apparently, you did. It said something about us being 'a fringe group who've set up their own laws.' Maybe you didn't know what you were signing, though. I know how busy you get. Maybe someone snuck it past you?"

The king looked angrily across the table at his prime minister. "Not cool, Haman. Not cool."

"Well, to be fair, I did tell you about this..." Haman explained.

"I thought you were going to

bust some Libertarians, not exterminate an entire race of people!" The king was incensed. "Great. Now I look like a total racist. Thanks a lot, Haman! Oh, I am so pig-biting mad right now! You'll both have to excuse me, I'm going outside to clear my head for a minute."

Seeing the king all roiled up like that terrified Haman.

"Please," he begged Esther, "if I had known that you were Jewish, I never would have...please... you've got to say something to him..."

Haman was groveling so hard that without even noticing what he was doing, he walked over to the couch and began pawing Esther. As if on cue, Xerxes came back into the room at this exact moment and saw Haman climbing all over his wife.

"What the HELL, dude?" The king said, seeing Haman lying on top of Esther. "You just don't know when to quit, do you?" At this point, it occurred to Haman that he had probably seen his last parade.

The king was so irate, he wanted to execute Haman in the most horribly memorable way possible. Luckily, there was a seventy-five foot spike lying around that did the trick. King Xerxes had Haman impaled on the spike, and made Mordecai his new prime minister.

"Here's the rub," the king explained. "I'm afraid my order to kill all the Jews still stands. Once I've put my seal to a new law, I can't take it back. But, what I CAN do is issue a second order to arm the Jews so they can kill anyone who tries to act on my first order. Sorry, I'm afraid that's the best I can do under the circumstances."

In the following weeks, a war raged between those trying to kill the Jews according to the king's first order and those trying to protect them according to his second order. All told, some seventy-five thousand people died as a result of this bureaucratic glitch.

"Well, let me say, this has certainly taught me a lesson about reading what I sign!" the king said.

It was a close call, but in the end, the Jewish people were saved from extermination by Esther's courage. And, in a strange way, by Vashti's refusal to give the king a lap dance.

GOD
HAS A THING FOR THE
MIDDLE EAST

PART THREE
WISDOM AND POETRY

In which God and Satan make a friendly wager, King David releases a greatest-hits album, and King Solomon teaches you how to treat a lady.

 EING KING AFFORDS YOU A LOT OF TIME TO THINK ABOUT life and jam on your harp. Collectively, David and Solomon wrote hundreds of Psalms, which were love poems to God, set to music. Sort of the ancient Jewish equivalent to Gospel music. Solomon also wrote hundreds of one-liners and bon-mots which became the Book of Proverbs. Not to mention some sexy poetry, for which he wrote both the male and female parts. Kinky. As an artistic choice, I took the liberty of presenting that book, The Song of Solomon, exclusively from the female point of view. I hope you don't mind.

An unnamed king, a descendant of Solomon and David's, wrote the Book of Ecclesiastes, an honest meditation on the paradox and futility of life, and very possibly the first work of existentialist philosophy.

Then there's the Book of Job, which attempts to answer the age-old question of why the innocent suffer. On the surface, the answer appears to be that God's got action riding on us. But in *The Guide for the Perplexed*, the medieval rabbi Maimonides offers a different possibility: Job, like the rest of us, must suffer because it means nothing to worship out of habit—praying and getting rewarded, like a dog who rolls over because he knows he's going to get a treat. Only when the treats are not forthcoming do we question our faith. And only then do we, like Job, discover what we truly believe.

THE BOOK OF JOB

 OD AND SATAN MAKE this crazy bet.

Satan claims that this guy named Job only loves God because God gave him wealth, respect and a large and adoring family. So to prove Satan wrong, God allows Satan to kill off Job's wife and kids and strip him of his wealth through a series of disasters. To top it all off, Satan is allowed to give Job all kinds of sores and diseases. He even makes Job stink. His friends and neighbors begin to wonder if hanging around Job might not be bad luck, so they stop coming by his house.

Finally, when Job hits rock bottom, he curses the day he was born. But even lonely, beaten and forced to sit in a bucket of ash all day to ease his sores, Job does not lose faith in God. Satan concedes the bet and gives God the supernatural equivalent of a twenty-dollar bill or whatever it was they agreed upon as their wager. God then rewards Job for his faith by giving him more money, smarter kids and a hotter wife than he ever had before.

"Okay, you won on Job," Satan said. "But twenty bucks says *that* guy will totally flip you off."

"Who, *that* guy?" God asked, looking into the distance.

"Care for a little bet to make things interesting?"

PSALMS

ING DAVID WAS the most famous harp player in history. His music is timeless. His songs have sold millions in Europe. Now, for the first time ever, all his greatest hits are compiled in one priceless collection! At last you can have all your old favorites right at your fingertips, including songs by his father Jesse, his son Solomon, and all the King David Family Singers. Includes such classics as:

The Lord Is My Shepherd (I Shall Not Want) **Psalm 23**

I'll Feed You Honey from a Rock **Psalm 81**

Weary with Sorrow (It'll Be Better Tomorrow) **Psalm 119**

Satisfy Me (With Your Finest Wheat) **Psalm 147**

The Tents of Kedar (Be Rockin' Tonight!) **Psalm 120**

"Requests? How about a psalm?
I've got a ton of them."

No artist has touched as many hearts or stood the test of time quite like King David. In this unique collection, you'll hear the songs that span his illustrious career and celebrate the changing times in which he lived. From his early days as a gospel act, to his maturing social consciousness as a folk legend...

The Righteous Will Laugh at the Rich (I Am an Olive Tree)
Psalm 52

Listen to the Needy Groan
Psalm 12

I Stand Alone (Surrounded By Bulls)
Psalm 22

Dwell in My Sacred Tent, Live on My Holy Mountain, Girl
Psalm 15

To his heavy metal phase...

You're Gonna Be Eaten By Dogs
Psalm 68

Teach the Children (About Death and Pain)
Psalm 78

Dwelling in Darkness (Please Destroy My Enemies)
Psalm 143

This collection even includes David's never before released hip-hop demos...

God Be Creepin' on a Fool
Psalm 109

Save Me, Lord (From Deez Ruthless Bitchez)
Psalm 86

Plus many, many more!

All the songs you see here— plus all the classics from the King David Family Singers—are gathered together for the first time in box-set form. These are the songs that we grew up to, the songs we worked to, and made love to. Now, at last, they're yours in one timeless collection.

THE BOOK OF PROVERBS

 HE **BOOK OF PROVERBS** is a collection of wise sayings written primarily by King Solomon. Much like a Kenny Rogers album, it's mostly advice about life, money, and how to treat a woman.

Some of the life lessons offered by Proverbs:

Don't sleep with another man's wife. A prostitute will only cost you a loaf of bread, but sleep with another guy's woman and you have to look over your shoulder for the rest of your life. You can't carry a fire in your heart without burning your chest.

Don't be a liar. A lie might taste sweet at first, but it's just a matter of time before it turns to gravel in your mouth.

Also, don't be one of those smug, entitled jerks who looks down on people who aren't as lucky as you are. When you belittle the poor, you make fun of God. But when you give money to the poor, you are lending it to God. If you laugh at the misfortunes of others, God will give them a chance to laugh at yours. So be cool.

Never miss a good opportunity to shut up. Smart guys don't feel the need to jabber all the time and dumb guys are only mistaken for smart when they aren't talking. An idiot is a bomb and his mouth is the fuse.

It's okay to admit you're wrong once in a while. How stupid you look when you're wrong is directly proportional to how certain you were that you were right. A wise man will always consider the possibility that he's wrong and he will welcome a second opinion. Only an asshole thinks his first guess is right every time.

Work hard and save up for hard times. An ant doesn't need to be told to work hard by his boss or the government, and neither should you. At the same time, don't knock yourself out trying to get rich. Money doesn't do you any good if you've wasted your whole life getting it. Money is a bird: just when you think you've got it cornered, it flutters away, making you look like a real prat as you jump after it.

If you are rich or powerful, don't drink too much. It will make you lazy, oppressive, and forgetful. If, on the other hand, you are destitute, miserable or dying…drink away. You probably need to do some forgetting.

A nation with corrupt rulers is a country always in rebellion. But deal honestly with the powerless and your throne will never be in danger. Putting a corrupt man in power is like releasing a bear in the town square. A dishonest man is always on the run, even when nobody's chasing him. But a man with integrity can stand his ground, even when all are against him.

Finding a good wife is better than discovering buried treasure.

Marrying a trophy wife without any common sense is like finding a gold ring in a pig's snout. You might get the gold ring, but it's not worth whatever you had to do to that pig to get it. A good wife is hard-working, smart with money, and keeps the house running smoothly. A good wife will make you look better than you really are. And guys, if you have a wife who makes you proud, the least you can do is let her know what she means to you.

A woman will forgive a lot of bullshit if you aren't cold and uncaring.

"Wow—these proverbs are great."

ECCLESIASTES

 PEAKING AS YOUR king, and as a descendant of King David, I hope you will indulge me if I philosophize a little. I've been around the block and have seen just about everything, and let me tell you: it's all horseshit. Everything you do, everything you'll ever accomplish, your life's work, your kids' life's work: horseshit. I mean, none of it matters.

The world will keep humming long after you and everything you've ever done is gone and forgotten. And nothing you can possibly do will change any of that. What can a man possibly hope to accomplish in the brief moment of sunshine that is a life?

Hey, that goes for me too, and I have a palace filled with naked concubines. I've got massive armies of soldiers and the wisest men in the world, just hanging around, eating my pineapple. Doesn't matter. The day will come when all that will be gone, I will be forgotten, and everything I ever did with my wealth and power will not have made one donkey turd's worth of difference to the world.

Everything's temporary. There's an occasion for everything you can think of. A time to be born, a time to die. A time to cry and a time to dance. A time for war and a time for peace. It's all happened before and it will all happen again. There's nothing new under the sun and nothing you do can change the heaving tide of history for more than a second or two. The world is nothing but a huge fad.

So if you can't change the world, you might as well make yourself happy, right? Nope. That's pointless, too. Gorging yourself with food just makes you gluttonous, filling your head with knowledge just makes you aware of your own ignorance, and hoarding money just makes you greedier. Service to God isn't a bad idea, just don't expect any reward for your efforts.

It doesn't matter how great you are, or how much of a legacy you think you have created for yourself, when all is said and done, you will die like everything else and that will be the end of you. It is better to be a living dog than a dead lion.

Trust me, it doesn't matter what you come up with to do with your life, in the end, it all turns to dust. You can't even take solace in knowing the truth.

The truth is that it's better to cry real tears than to fake laughter. Better to be a sinner who surprises himself with goodness than a righteous man who disappoints himself with sin. Better to be condemned by a wise man than praised by idiots. How is anyone supposed to make sense of the truth?

It's enough to make one cynical, I know, but don't give in to cynicism just yet. For I will let you in on one more secret I've discovered during my long and meaningless lifetime:

Just because life is pointless, that doesn't mean you get to sit around all day moaning about it. There's still work to be done. You should still help the oppressed, take care of the abandoned, and make each other happy if and when you can. Just because there's no point to any of it doesn't mean it's not the right thing to do.

"He's humming 'Dust in the Wind' again."

SONG OF SONGS
(AKA SONG OF SOLOMON)

 HE KING IS SO HOT. I love it when he gives me one of his "palace tours" that ends in the bedroom. Although, it's a little embarrassing, walking around the palace. Everyone stares at me because I'm so tanned and poor and it's obvious to all of them I'm just some chick who works in the fields. But I don't care. Let them stare. Maybe they need to see what a happy woman looks like.

The king is so sweet. And did I mention that he's hot? He lets me eat in the banquet hall and he feeds me raisins and apples. And on top of it all, he's an amazing kisser. I'm going to faint just thinking about him! Last night, I kept waking up, wishing he were in my bed. When morning came, I went into town, just so I could catch a glimpse of him. He was riding around in his golden carriage with, like, sixty bodyguards. He's such a showoff!

Did I tell you what he said to me the other night? He said my eyes were like doves and my hair was like a flock of goats. Oh. My. God. I thought I was going to melt! He said my teeth were like sheep (don't ask, he has a thing about animal metaphors) and that my boobs were like a pair of gazelles. I'm pretty sure that was meant as a compliment. And then (I think I'm going to explode!), he asked me to go away with him! He said my love was his wine and my body was his fruit. Let's just say there was a lot of wine and fruit tasting going on that night.

When the morning came, I felt like I never wanted to leave or get dressed. I just wanted to stay in bed with him forever. But when I rolled over to say good morning, he was already gone. The palace staff totally turned on me once the king had left. They beat me, tore my clothes and gave me the bum's rush out of the palace. I don't care, though, that ivory body and those sweet lips have me wanting more.

I ran into him later, and again he went on about how my love was wine, my hair was goats and my body was fruit (in fact, he went straight for my clusters of grapes, if you know what I mean). Again, he asked me to leave town with him. He said that he wished he could be more in the open about our relationship, that he could introduce me to his mother. I don't know if he's serious or if he's just feeding me a line, and frankly, I don't care. I'm in love and not even a river can wash that feeling away. Oh, I know this has almost no chance of ending well, but I can endure anything if I can just be in love while doing it.

PART FOUR
THE MAJOR PROPHETS

*In which Isaiah gets work as a motivational speaker,
Jeremiah's poetry submissions are rejected, and Ezekiel is the
victim of an alien abduction.*

 HE SALAD DAYS WERE OVER. GOD WAS FEELING HURT AND betrayed by his chosen people. The tiny Jewish kingdoms of Israel and Judah were surrounded on three sides by the superpowers of the ancient world: Egypt, Babylon, and Assyria. The only question seemed to be which of these three empires they would be conquered by. This is where the prophets came in. Other than Isaiah, whose advice was actually sought by the government, most of the prophets were guys who just wandered in from the desert to tell the kings how awful and incompetent they were. This represented a shift in the literary culture.

Before, during the boom times, the kings snapped up the literate men and put them to work as scribes: keeping records, writing histories, telling the world how great the kings were. Once the kingdoms became two petty puppet states, and there was no more cheese in the cupboard for struggling writers, the literary culture totally changed. Now, the writing was coming from disgruntled prophets, eating crickets and self-publishing their pamphlets in the desert.

Needless to say, the prophets weren't very popular. They usually ended up being rode out of town on a camel, or dumped down a well.

One book which doesn't really fit that mold is Daniel. Daniel was written hundreds of years after the events it describes. It was written during the Greek occupation of Israel, not the earlier Babylonian occupation in which it takes place. The Greeks were always pressuring the Jews to assimilate. They banned circumcised dudes from the gymnasiums and outlawed kosher diets. As such, Daniel was probably written to be an after-school special to teach fellow Jews the value of resisting the pressure to worship Greek gods, or to have reconstructive surgery on their penises in hopes of getting a gym membership.

ISAIAH

HE **KING OF JUDAH** walked up to the podium and addressed his advisers.

"Okay, can everybody hear me? As you all know, Israel has been conquered by the Assyrians, meaning that we are now the sole remaining Jewish kingdom. As you can see from the situation map, we have the Assyrians coming down at us from the north, the Babylonians heading straight for us from the east, and then we got the Egyptians coming up from the south. Basically, we're caught in the middle of a Sumerian standoff between the three most powerful empires in the world. Needless to say, things are… uh, things are a little iffy. So to give us some much needed confidence, I have asked a motivational prophet to come speak to us today. Let's all give a warm welcome to the Prophet Isaiah."

(Applause.)

"I want you all to be honest with me," Isaiah asked, looking for

"I really hope the Messiah lets us keep imported beer."

a show of hands, "how many of you feel like *winners*? Not many, huh? Well, I can understand why. You all saw the shit-stomping Israel got and you're wondering 'Are we next?' You're surrounded on all sides by enemies bigger and stronger than yourself. Why wouldn't you be scared?

"But I'm here to tell each and every one of you that YOU ARE A WINNER! Not because of anything you've done. Not because you're rich, or powerful, or have a full head of hair. No, you're winners for one reason and one reason only...you are God's chosen people.

"And how does a winner behave? A winner acts like he belongs. He doesn't cower. He doesn't find a daddy to protect him. He stands on his own two feet. I've seen scared nations before and I know what they do. They curry favor. They adopt foreign gods. They make alliances with foreign nations that don't have their best interest at heart, and then they're surprised when their protectors turn on them.

"I'm going to say this just once: you CANNOT trust foreigners to protect you. If you join forces with one of these empires and it loses a war to one of the others, the winner is going to see us

as a hostile nation and invade. And even if you join forces with the winning empire, once it realizes it no longer needs you, *it* will invade.

"Let me see if I can put this in terms anyone can understand: There is a chicken named Judah. This unlucky chicken happens to live in a cul de sac where its neighbors are an alligator, a lion and a coyote. Judah the chicken would like to go on living. Who should he trust to save him? A) The alligator. B) The lion. C) The coyote or D) the Almighty God. As naive as this may sound to you, the answer is actually D. The chicken should trust in God. And do you know why? Because God is the only choice WHO DOESN'T EAT CHICKEN!

"Nobody respects a loser, and a winner does not beg for protection. So the only way to convince people you're a winner is to stand tall. It's not camel-science, people!

"But, Isaiah, you might ask, suppose they do invade us. How do I convince God to save us from annihilation? I can't even convince my wife to give me a foot rub!"

(Laughter.)

"The answer, as always, is simple: you get God to save you by being a people worth saving. All God wants from you, all he's ever wanted, is your love and respect. Now, some of you believe that God is just one among many gods. So you feel like you can choose to worship him or some idol the same way you would pick out a hat to wear to a party. And many of you who stay true to God only do so because you think he's better than the other gods. Well, at the risk of shocking you, I'm here to tell you that Jehovah is not just the best god, he's the ONLY god!

"I have news for you. When you have to carve an idol out of balsa wood so it can tell you what to do, you're not worshiping a god. You're worshiping a puppet. You have to question the intelligence of someone who worships a god he made in shop class. A man who whittles a god out of a tree branch and then uses the rest of the tree for firewood has two things: a pile of firewood and crap. If anything, he should worship the firewood, at least that will keep him warm at night.

"But at least the heathens don't know any better. How you people, after witnessing God save your broccoli in the desert, after seeing him lead you out of Egypt and perform miracles before your very eyes, how you keep betting on golden calves and wooden idols is the real mystery.

"So, in summary, it doesn't make sense to make deals with any foreign rulers. You're merely choosing who gets to eat you. If you don't want to be eaten, then make your alliance with God. Put away your idols, show God some respect, and everything will be bananas foster. And remember: YOU. ARE. A. WINNER. Thank you all and goodnight!"

Isaiah pumped his fist in the air and walked off the stage to raucous applause. Everyone poured to the front of the room to shake his hand. The king thanked him for coming by. Once Isaiah had left the room, the door was closed and the king turned to his advisers.

"Pretty great, huh?" the king asked.

"Yeah, that guy was amazing!"

"So, what do you think? Should we take Isaiah's advice?" The king asked.

"Are you nuts? We *have* to make an alliance. He's a great motivational prophet and all, but come on, we have to live in the real world. Divine Intervention isn't a foreign policy."

So the king called up the Assyrians and made a deal. Judah became a puppet state, and the king basically became the regional manager of a hot and dusty corner of the

Assyrian Empire. As Isaiah predicted, this arrangement didn't work out very well. Before long, both Assyria and Judah were conquered by Babylon. The Babylonians carted away Judah's treasure and led the Jews away in chains.

"Well, you win some and you lose some," Isaiah mused. "Despite it all, I'm still pretty optimistic. God didn't choose us as his people, give us laws, and bring us out of Egypt just so we could serve drinks and carry fruit trays in Babylon.

He chose us so the rest of the world could know God.

"Someday we'll return to our homeland. Someday, a woman will give birth to a child named 'Immanuel,' who will free us from foreign rule. He'll be a wise king, the sort of king who listens to somebody whose job title is 'Prophet.' Someday, we won't have any kings at all. God will rule the Earth and put an end to all this war, corruption and greed.

"Someday," Isaiah sighed.

"Everything is crap, you know? There will be horrible wars and everyone will die. People are off worshiping false gods. It sucks. What's the point? Why get married and have kids if it's all just going to suck? Am I bumming you out?"

JEREMIAH

THE LAST YEARS OF Judah's existence were a precarious time. The great empires of the world were closing in on their tiny little borders, and their future as an independent nation was in grave doubt. Yet everyone wanted to believe that God would save them and that, somehow, everything would turn out all right.

Unfortunately, God appointed a prophet named Jeremiah for the sole purpose of strangling these hopes. God told Jeremiah to spread the word that his people had become a bunch of libertine, idolatrous pigs and that unless they changed their ways, they were doomed.

While Jeremiah was preaching in Jerusalem, there was an interesting development at the Temple. Cleaning out the basement, somebody found a dusty, old book. It happened to be the Book of Deuteronomy, which had mysteriously gone missing a few centuries earlier.

"Holy nuts, look at all these laws," the priests said. "We haven't been doing any of this shit!"

Jeremiah took the rediscovery of the Book of Deuteronomy as a good sign. "So that's the rock in God's shoe," Jeremiah thought. "We simply forgot a bunch of the laws. Once we start following the laws of Deuteronomy again, everything will be okay."

To Jeremiah's relief, the king reintroduced the laws of Deuteronomy with great fanfare, and a massive media campaign. Once people learned about the hundreds of new laws on the books, they wasted no time in ignoring them. Jeremiah was disgusted. He gave up on saving his people. Instead, he moped around, telling everyone to prepare themselves for the end. "We had our chance to save ourselves," Jeremiah said. "We chose pork cutlets instead."

Jeremiah would stand in the street and shout in graphic detail how the Kingdom of Judah would be obliterated by the Babylonians, how corpses would litter the fields like cowshit and how everyone they knew would soon be killed or enslaved. His sermons were not exactly crowd-pleasers.

Jeremiah hated being a prophet. He would have liked nothing more than to have been a well-adjusted, corn-fed patriot, like most of his countrymen.

But he couldn't help himself. He suffered from a sort of divine Tourette's syndrome. Somebody would run into a bar and announce that their wife had just given birth to a son. He'd try to smile and give them congratulations, but his mouth would say, "You know that baby's just going to die, don't you? Just because they're called Baby-lonians doesn't mean they like babies. This time next year, that baby will probably be impaled on a pitchfork or burned in a bonfire. That's why I'm not having any babies."

People would be minding their own business in the market square, when out of the blue, Jeremiah would smash a clay jar and shout, "That's what the Babylonians are going to do to us!"

He built a wooden yoke and wore it around town like an ox to symbolize the fact that they were all going to become pack animals for the mighty Babylonians.

Jeremiah would go to the Temple and interrupt people's prayers.

"Hey, what are you guys doing? Are you praying? Don't bother. God isn't fooled. Can a leopard change its spots? Can an Ethiopian turn white? You might be sorry today, but God knows that when tomorrow comes, you'll go right back to worshiping snakes. Feel free to keep coming to the Temple, though, there's some great sandwiches in the food court."

When he saw a group of guys talking politics, he would butt in, saying, "The Babylonians are way too strong for us. If we try to fight them, we're going to be devoured faster than goat cheese at a farmers' market."

Finally, when they'd had enough, the people threw Jeremiah down a well.

"That's for not supporting the troops!" someone shouted down at him.

It wasn't safe for Jeremiah to show his face in public anymore, so he began sending nasty letters via messenger. Sometimes, he'd have his messenger read his letters aloud to the king:

"God is going to destroy your kingdom. The Babylonians will enslave your children and use you for target practice. They'll destroy the Temple and help themselves to the holy treasure. They'll leave you lying in the dirt, so the crows can peck out your eyes and dogs can gnaw at your feet," the messenger read.

"Why do I keep letting that guy in here?" the king muttered to himself.

Jeremiah was the most hated man in Judah, but his unpopularity didn't make him any less right. The Babylonians did invade the Kingdom of Judah. They did crush Judah's armies and enslave its people. They destroyed the Temple, set Jerusalem aflame and stole everything that wasn't too heavy to haul away.

The Babylonians clapped Jeremiah in chains, along with thousands of his countrymen, and led them away toward Babylon. As they trundled down the road, the commander of the Babylonian army recognized Jeremiah.

"Hey, you're Jeremiah, aren't you? We heard about all the great things you said about us. You know, Babylon is not only a great empire, but a powerful force for good in the world. I wish more of you could see that…You know what? You should come to Babylon as our guest. We'll put you up in style, let you have any house you want. Maybe we'll even send you on a goodwill tour."

"I didn't shout in the streets about the destruction of my people because I love Babylon! I did it because they needed to know the truth. If you really want to do me a favor, let me stay here," Jeremiah said. "My people may hate me, but they're still my people."

The Babylonians shrugged, unshackled Jeremiah, and left him there among the ruins of his homeland.

"Bless you."

LAMENTATIONS

FTER THE BABYLONIANS destroyed Jerusalem and hauled away thousands of his countrymen to live in captivity, Jeremiah became so depressed that he crawled into a nearby cave and started writing bad high school poetry.

ODE TO A FAILED PROPHET (GRAVEL FACE)

God has broken my bones
Withered me up like an old man
And mauled me like a bear
Just for laughs.

He broke my teeth with rocks
And made me drink various body fluids
Before trampling me in the dust.

My own people hunted me down
They threw me into a pit
And while I lay there dying
They wrote parody songs about me.

Not my best day.

"Making you miserable is God's way of saying 'I love you.'"

WELCOME TO THE LAIR OF TORMENT

I shall summon a demon
sayeth the Lord with glee
to devour their castles from below
and swallow soldiers as they flee

and all your beautiful people
will no longer enjoy their fame
perhaps this is because their faces
have been licked off by dragon flame!

and oh, how the children shall weep
when there is no wine to slake their thirst
widowed mothers will starve to death
…but they'll eat their babies first!

and oh, how the fool shall dance as they die
and laugh as they bleed
needless to say, the Lair of Torment
is a pretty messed up place, indeed!

REQUIEM FOR A PROM QUEEN

The once-beautiful city now lies empty and alone
Like a queen
Like a widow
Like a slave

Her tiara is broken
Her dress is stained
Tears carve into her cheeks like canyons
And no one's even there to ignore her

Her mom is out of town
Her boyfriend is gone
And her friends
Were never really her friends

If a heart breaks
And nobody's around to hear it
Does it make a sound?

Jeremiah emerged from his cave to read his poetry to the people, at which point they kidnapped him and sent him to Egypt.

EZEKIEL

OD WAS WAITING BY the phone. He was getting desperate. He and the Jews had been broken up for a while now, and he was beginning to worry that they might never call. So God sent some prophets to scare the Jews into coming back to him.

Ezekiel was sitting in the desert one day when saw a large metallic wheel descend through the clouds. It was inhabited by strange, human-like creatures which had a different face on each side of their head. These creatures gave Ezekiel a scroll, but instead of reading it, they told him to eat it. Surprisingly, it didn't taste all that bad.

After his encounter with the UFO, and the light snack which followed, Ezekiel began to hear the voice of God.

God's voice boomed at Ezekiel, telling him to go to Jerusalem and warn the people that disaster was coming, that soon they would all be destroyed.

"They probably won't listen to you," God explained. "We were together for centuries, and let me tell you, they are terrible listeners. So we're going to have to get a little funky to grab their attention.

Okay, Ezekiel is it? Ezekiel, here's what I want you to do: while you're preaching to them, I want you to tie yourself up with ropes and lie on your left side for three hundred and ninety-days in a row. Then, turn over and lie on your right side for another forty days. One day to symbolize each year they've been living in sin."

"Won't I die?" Ezekiel asked.

"Good point. You'd better take a lunch. No, even better: take some flour, and then bake your own bread over a big, burning pile of human excrement. That will totally blow their minds."

"I don't think I want to do that," Ezekiel protested.

"Okay, fine, bake it over some cow dung, then."

"I'm still not entirely on board with this concept."

"Listen Ezekiel, I really need you to get on board with this, otherwise, I've just got to wipe them all out without giving them a chance to repent. You wouldn't want that on your conscience, would you?"

"I suppose not."

Ezekiel dutifully went to Jerusalem, and tied himself up in ropes. He lay on his side for over a year, all the while eating bread baked with cow shit. Word spread throughout the land about Ezekiel and his unique brand of showmanship.

"He did *what*?" people would say. "That's disgusting! Where's he performing next week?"

For his next show, God told Ezekiel to stand in the middle of the town square and shave off all his hair with a sword.

"I want you to grab a handful of your hair and set it on fire. Then grab another handful and stab it with your sword. Finally, scoop up the rest of your hair and toss it into the wind."

"What's that supposed to accomplish?"

"It's symbolism," God explained. "Everyone loves symbolism. Trust me."

Again, Ezekiel did as he was told. As he shaved his head with a sword, he told the people that without God's protection, the city of Jerusalem would soon be besieged and destroyed.

"The dead will litter the streets and clog the rivers. Mothers will eat their children and children will eat their mothers. Many of you will die in the fire, or be put to the sword, and those who survive will be scattered to the winds to live like refugees."

The crowd erupted into cheers.

"Did you see what that nut did to his hair?"

"We'll be scattered to the wind...just like that hair. Hey, I get it!" someone shouted. "We're Ezekiel's hair!"

"We're Ezekiel's hair! We're Ezekiel's hair!" the crowd chanted.

The curse of being a really great showman is that you're never sure whether people come to hear what you have to say, or just to see what you're going to do next. No matter what Ezekiel did to drive the point home to them, people seemed to just enjoy the show and then went right on worshiping idols, eating forbidden meats, and doing all the things that made God feel jealous and unloved.

Bald and frustrated, Ezekiel decided to give the theatrics a rest and focus on his message. He stood before a crowd and told them a parable about a man who had two slutty daughters. One of the daughters had a thing for Assyrian men. She would sleep with any guy who had an Assyrian accent. The other daughter liked Babylonian men, who were "hung like a donkey and could cum like a horse."[1] Eventually when the father found out about his girls' extra-curricular activities, he threw them out of the house

[1] EZEKIEL 23:20

and let anyone who wanted to have his way with them.

"That'll teach them to be sluts!" the father said.

The father, of course, was a thinly veiled version of God, and the two horny daughters were Israel and Judah, the two Jewish kingdoms. But the meaning was lost on an indifferent audience.

"Tell us more about the horse!" they shouted.

"I think I know what the problem is," God said afterward.

"What's that?" Ezekiel asked.

"There needs to be an emotional component to your stories," God explained. "Something that will allow the listener to relate to you directly. I know just the trick! I'm going to kill your wife."

"What?"

"Keep your turban on. Just hear me out. When you've lost the person you love most in the world, then you can really drive the point home with them. Tell them that if I killed my own prophet's wife, imagine what I would do to their loved ones. It lets them know I mean business!"

Somewhere in the distance, Ezekiel's wife was tending her goats when she suddenly toppled over and died.

Ezekiel warned the people once again, telling them about his dead wife.

"My wife is dead," he told them. "She had absolutely nothing to do with any of this, and yet, God killed her just to get to me. And he *likes* me. So what do you think he'll do to you, if you don't change your ways?"

Once again, Ezekiel was ignored. God finally gave up on the idea that his people were ever going to come back to him. He was ready to move on. God withdrew his protection, letting the Babylonians storm into Jerusalem and kill everyone they could find. They razed the Temple and set fire to the city.

Ezekiel was depressed. His wife was dead. His country lay in ruins. His people had been sent away into exile. God woke Ezekiel up amidst the rubble and destruction.

"What do you want now?" Ezekiel asked.

"One last thing, Ezekiel, I promise. You do this for me and you're done."

God led Ezekiel to a battlefield littered with bones and told him to bring the bones back to life.

"Bones! I command you to come back to life!"

"Well, you don't have to be a dick about it!" God said, "Just ask them nicely."

"Bones," Ezekiel said, "please come back to life, if you would?"

"That's better!"

The bones in the field slowly began to come together to form into skeletons. The skeletons stood up, drowsy from years of sleep. Tendons and muscles soon began to grow over the sun-parched white of the bones, and then they were in turn covered by skin and clothes and armor until Ezekiel saw a vast army standing in front of him.

"You see how easy that was?" God asked. "This is the fallen army of Israel. You're upset with me because I killed your wife, let the Babylonians destroy your city, and reduced your people to slavery. I get that. But that's small beer, son. You're thinking like a man, not like a god. You see? Look at how easily I can put all that back together again.

"Don't worry, this story isn't over by a long shot. I'll fix the nation of Israel. I'll bring Jerusalem back to life, just like I did this army. I'll even rebuild the Temple. The only difference is that next time around, people will appreciate it more, because they'll know what it's like to be scattered, to be separated from their homes, their people, and their God."

As they walked away, God told Ezekiel about his plans. "When we rebuild Jerusalem, I'm thinking we might go for a nice, symmetrical design. Long, straight streets. That'll be a good look, don't you think?"

"So we'll just wait here, then?" asked one of the ghost soldiers, as God and Ezekiel disappeared into the distance.

DANIEL

RUNNING A GLOBAL empire is a serious business. You need administrators, advisors, viceroys, and satraps. You can never have too many satraps. To ensure that they always had a large and competent executive class, the Babylonians designed a school specifically to train young men to rule the world. It was sort of like Yale. Among those enrolled in the school were four promising Jewish boys named Daniel, Shadrach, Meschach, and Abednego.

Now, this school had the best cafeteria food in the history of higher education. Every morning, they put out a massive feast of roast pig, stuffed peacock, quail eggs, wine, and unlimited breadsticks. Despite all the amazing food, though, Daniel and his friends refused to eat there because they didn't have a kosher menu. Instead, they ate raw carrots and salad in their dorm room, which they washed down with water.

The Babylonians weren't entirely sold on the boys' vegan diet, but they dropped the matter when they saw how chiseled, sexy, and smart they turned out to be.

In addition to being strong, good-looking, and brilliant, Daniel also developed a knack for interpreting dreams, which in the ancient world, really put you on the fast track to success.

King Nebuchadnezzar had a dream which really shook him up. He summoned all his advisors and magicians to interpret the dream, which normally wouldn't have been a problem, except that he wouldn't tell them what the dream was.

"This is the only way I can be sure your interpretation is coming from the gods," he explained, "rather than just some pop psychology bullshit you picked up in college."

When nobody could tell him what his dream was, Nebuchadnezzar threatened to have his entire council executed.

"But I'm a foreign policy expert!" one of them protested.

Luckily for the council, Daniel stepped in and revealed that Nebuchadnezzar had been dreaming about an enormous statue.

"Go on," the king said.

"The statue's head was made of gold, its chest and arms were made out of silver, its midsection was

made out of bronze, and its legs were cast from iron. The statue's feet were made out of clay. Then a giant boulder rolled into the statue, shattering it into a hundred pieces."

Everyone held their breath, waiting for the king's reply.

"That's it. That was my dream. But what does it mean?"

Daniel explained that the statue's golden head represented Babylon. Babylon would someday be defeated and replaced by another empire, represented by the somewhat less impressive silver chest. This empire would itself be defeated, and its successors would in turn be replaced by increasingly corrupt and dysfunctional nations, until one day when God would come down like a boulder, smashing all the kingdoms so that he could rule

the entire world as the Kingdom of God.

"Well, I don't take a lot of solace in those predictions," the king said, "but at least now I can put this whole dream business behind me, and focus on the company picnic."

King Nebuchadnezzar threw an enormous company picnic for all the satraps, governors, and middle managers of the Babylonian Empire. As a team-building exercise, he decided to have everyone bow down to the same giant idol at the same time.

"This is a very simple game," Nebuchadnezzar explained. "When the music plays, start bowing! To add to the fun, we have constructed this blazing furnace so that anyone who doesn't bow will be burned alive. Okay, everybody ready?"

The flutes and the drums struck up and, on cue, everyone bowed down to the statue.

"Hey, the Jews are cheating!" somebody complained.

Nebuchadnezzar looked over and saw Shadrach, Meshach, and Abednego, still standing while everyone else was bowing. He called them over.

"Look, maybe you guys didn't understand the rules. When the music starts playing, you're supposed to bow down to that statue over there. Otherwise, I got to throw you into this furnace. Got it?"

"I understand the rules," one of them said, "and believe me, if I'd thought there was any chance of getting incinerated at the company picnic, I would have called in sick. But our God won't let us bow down to idols, and frankly, I'm more afraid of him than I am of you."

When Nebuchadnezzar heard this, he snapped. He ordered his servants to stoke the furnace before throwing the trouble-makers in. "I'll show you some team-building!" he barked as the servants stoked the furnace. The fire was so hot now that the soldiers disintegrated as they threw the three men into the flame.

Inside the furnace, Shadrach, Meshach, and Abednego, stood miraculously unharmed. They waited there, enjoying the heat until Nebuchadnezzar ordered his servants to fish them out. They emerged from the furnace without a single hair out of place. King Nebuchadnezzar was so impressed by their devotion to their god, and by his devotion to them, that he welcomed Shadrach, Meshach, and Abednego back into the land of the non-burning and rewarded them all with nice fat promotions. Surviving an execution was also a good way to get ahead in those days.

Not long after the thing with the furnace, Nebuchadnezzar was walking around his balcony, taking in the Hanging Gardens, when he suddenly went insane. For the next seven years, he lived like a wild man, growing a feathery, totally out-of-control beard and fingernails like bird claws. He would run around on all fours and tear grass out of the ground with his teeth, and people would say, "Hey, didn't that guy used to be king?"

After he went crazy, Nebuchadnezzar's son Belshazzar took over ruling the Babylonian Empire. At one of his dinner parties, he thought it would be fun to eat off the holy goblets and plates the Babylonians had stolen from the Temple in Jerusalem. Halfway through the dinner, a large phantom hand appeared in mid-air and began writing strange words on the wall. This bothered the king so much that he summoned Daniel to make sense of the writing.

Daniel told Belshazzar that using the holy dinnerware made God extremely upset and that, consequently, his reign would be coming to an end that very night. God doesn't like people using his cup.

During dinner, Babylon was conquered in a sneak attack by the Persians, and Belshazzar was thrown out like bad cheese.

As the new ruler of Babylon, the Persian King Darius was so impressed with Daniel, and his abilities to interpret dreams and supernatural graffiti, that he announced his intention to make him second-in-command over his entire empire. This made everyone else in the Babylonian civil service extremely jealous. They were all facing layoffs as a result of their merger with the Persian Empire, but now the new guy was going to be the Vice Emperor?

"Daniel? The dream guy?" they asked incredulously.

It was even worse for the Persian ruling class, who'd spent their whole lives climbing the corporate ladder.

"Thirty years and I'm still the Associate Vice President in Charge of Cups and Bowls," one of them complained. "Now, suddenly, some prisoner of war is going to get the number two job? I'm shitting pure rage right here!"

So a group of Daniel's disgruntled co-workers got together and hatched a crafty plan. After seeing the stunt Shadrach, Meshach, and Abednego had pulled during the company picnic, they knew that Daniel's religion wouldn't allow him to worship another god.

So they went to King Darius and said, "You know what, King? You've been working so hard, and doing such a great job, we all think you deserve a little treat. How about this? For the next month, everyone in the whole empire will have to pray only to you. And just to make it official, we'll pass a law which says that anyone who worships another god during that time will be dropped into a pit of lions. What do you think of that?"

"Well," the King said, "that does sound pretty nice. If you all think it's a good idea, I suppose it would be okay."

Despite the new law, every morning Daniel would kneel toward Jerusalem and pray to God, just as he had done his entire life. The advisers, peeping through Daniel's window, called the police the moment he began praying. King Darius was annoyed. He had no idea that Daniel's religion would trap him into violating the law.

"I *thought* that was kind of a weird suggestion," the king said. "I'm so sorry, Daniel, I let myself get tricked into signing this stupid law. But unfortunately, stupid or not, it is the law. Once I sign it, even I have to obey the law."

Having offered his apology, the king had Daniel lowered into the pit of lions. King Darius went home, but was too bummed thinking about Daniel getting torn apart by lions to enjoy his evening snack or watch his dancing girls. "I think I'm just going to go to bed," he announced glumly.

The next morning, he got up and went down to the lions' den, expecting to mop up whatever was left of his friend and protégé. Instead, he found Daniel alive and unscratched. God had spared Daniel just as he had saved Shadrach, Meshach, and Abednego from the team-building exercise.

The king had Daniel hoisted out of the lions' den. Then, to teach them a lesson, he threw the advisers who'd tricked him into the pit of lions, along with their wives and children. The lions immediately devoured them and everyone had a good laugh.

Despite the fact that he was a Jew in the Persian Empire, Daniel never stopped dreaming. Literally. He began keeping a dream log, which was soon filled with apocalyptic visions of the future and the end of the world. In his dreams, the Jews would be allowed to return to Israel. They would rebuild the Temple. Then they'd be invaded again. The next nation to occupy Israel would put an end to animal sacrifices at the Temple and, three and a half years later, the world would come to an end. The important thing was the Jews had to keep the faith, even as the whole world crumbled around them.

PART FIVE
THE MINOR PROPHETS

In which we learn the bright side of marrying a whore, God punches many things, and the wicked are set on fire.

 HE **MINOR PROPHETS ARE SORT OF LIKE THE BIBLE'S AM** radio dial. They were constantly railing against the government and complaining about how the nation had lost its moral compass. These prophets were uniquely blessed with the ability to see everything wrong about everyone else. The Minor Prophets basically existed to give Israel poor body image.

In their defense, they lived during anxious times. The Minor Prophets wrote after Israel had been split into two kingdoms: Israel and Judah. Some of the books were written just before the two kingdoms were conquered, respectively, by Assyria and Babylon. Some were written after they were conquered, while the Jews were forced to live in captivity. Others were written after the Jews were allowed to return to Israel. Regardless of when they were written, the Minor Prophets had one consistent theme: something is about to go horribly wrong, and it's all your fault.

HOSEA

OSEA WAS A PROPHET whose wife was always cheating on him. Every day, Hosea would go out into the town square and call upon the people of Israel to change their ways.

"You've turned your backs on the Laws of Moses!" he'd shout. "You've been worshiping pagan gods, and giving the sacred raisin cakes to your idols, WHEN YOU KNOW THOSE ARE GOD'S FAVORITE!"

But his words would be lost on the crowd because everyone was snickering. They all knew that while he was preaching, his wife, Gomer, was somewhere getting boned by a sailor or a stonemason or some swarthy goat herder.

At the end of each day, Hosea would pack up his pedestal and his tip jar and return home to find his wife missing. Knowing what she was up to, Hosea would stomp through the streets looking for her. When he found Gomer, they'd created a huge scene in the middle of the street, much to the amusement of the people of Israel.

But the next day, Hosea would be back in the marketplace, condemning the people's idolatry and general lack of enthusiasm for being Jews. Once again, his words were ignored as the crowd began laughing at Hosea, the cuckold.

Hosea and Gomer had three children. Or, I should say, Gomer had three children, as Hosea wasn't the father of any of them. Sometimes she'd disappear with a new lover for months at a time, but inevitably the romance would sour, or her new lover would get tired of her and throw her out into the street. Every time, she came crawling home, and Hosea always took her back. One time, she ran off with a guy who decided to make a few extra shekels by selling her off as a slave. In what had to be an all-time low, even for Hosea, he actually had to pay his wife's lover in order to buy her back.

People could not believe that Hosea would put up with Gomer after all the times she'd stepped out on him. Hosea was back in the town square preaching when someone finally worked up the nerve to ask him why he didn't simply throw his wife out on her ass.

Hosea shrugged, saying that his relationship with his wife was like God's relationship with us. That we are always cheating on God, leaving him for some sexy new idol or chasing some fleeting object of desire, but no matter how badly we break his heart or ridiculous we make him feel, he is always prepared to swallow his pride and take us back.

And the people finally understood what Hosea had been preaching about the whole time.

"My wife is a lying cheating whore, but she makes for a great metaphor."

JOEL

DEAR **ISRAEL,**

Have I got a prophecy for you! It mostly involves grasshoppers. Because you've screwed up God's plan for you so badly, he has decided to push the red button, wipe your country off the face of the Earth and start over from scratch.

This is how the end will come:

Locusts will eat your crops. Then there will be a horrible drought. People will die of thirst.

Your fields will turn to dust, and the quality of your olive oil will definitely suffer. But that's just the beginning. The grass will dry up, the streams will disappear, and all the little sheep and cows will turn their heads towards heaven and cry for rain. Doesn't that image just break your heart?

On the other hand, I also have a much nicer prophecy to share with you: if you all repent and start living the way Moses taught you, God will forgive you.

"Your problems call for a national day of prayer."

If you apologize to God, give up bacon and put away your idols, the rain will come back. Your crops will grow. Your fruit will taste better than ever. Your cows and sheep will stop their crying. Your kids will become prophets. Your old people will have these really amazing dreams.

All the foreigners will go back to wherever the hell they came from. Egypt will dry up like a prune.

The Assyrians will watch as their sons become male prostitutes. Wine will start flowing from the mountains in rivulets, and little streams of milk will start trickling through the hills.

All you have to do is say you're sorry and go back to him.

Signed,

The Prophet Joel

AMOS

 MOS WAS A SHEPHERD who moonlighted as a prophet. He also did a little tree surgery on the side. During Amos' time, Israel was at peace and its economy was starting to really take off. But amidst these boom times, Amos was disturbed by the greed and moral decay he saw all around him. The people of Israel had become soft and cosmopolitan. They sat on Corinthian leather, drank imported wine, and worshiped the most expensive gods. Those who couldn't hack it in the new economy were dumped into the streets to starve to death.

People who had once owned their own land were forced to become farmhands. Farmers who once grew all their own food now planted vineyards and became insufferable wine snobs. Amos didn't like the fact that a once-united people were being increasingly divided into rich plantation owners and destitute farmhands.

A people only gain sophistication at the expense of their identity. And Amos worried that the Jews were in danger of becoming one more drunken tribe of pagans, living off the hard work of slaves.

"If we're going to be just like

the pagans," Amos wondered, "why should God bother protecting us?"

"God will do what he can to rescue Israel," Amos warned people, "but when you pull a sheep from the jaws of a lion, sometimes all you get back are a couple of legs. Or an ear. So even if he does save us, we might not all make it."

"What do I have to worry about?" somebody would argue. "I sing in the choir. I make my sacrifices every month. Surely if God saves anyone, he'll save me."

"Do you think God cares about your hymns?" Amos replied. "Do you think he needs your goat meat? God doesn't give a heavenly shit about your church camps or your animal sacrifices as long as you're evicting his people from their homes and letting his children wander the streets hungry."

A pair of affluent men stepped up to argue with Amos.

"Maybe God rewards the righteous with money. You ever stop to think about that? Maybe all these poor people are loafers being punished by God for their laziness. Maybe we'd make God angry if we try to help people he has cursed with poverty."

"Hey, that's good," the man's friend said, sipping a goblet of wine. "You should start a newsletter!"

"So if somebody gets rich taking

"God wants you to be rich, and by that, I mean God wants me to be rich."

bribes or foreclosing on some old widow's farm, you think that's *proof* of their holiness?" Amos asked. "And if they sell the widow's children to a salt mine, those kids must have had it coming? What planet do you live on?"

Amos continued. "Believe it or not, God didn't bring you out of the desert just so you could cheat and rob each other. God isn't rewarding you, he is *disgusted* with you. God would rather burn the whole country to the ground than watch you swindle people and imagine your greed to be the mark of his approval."

Amos upset a lot of people, so it wasn't long before the king summoned him to the palace.

"Amos, buddy, why do you want to rock the apple cart?" the king said, rubbing Amos' shoulders in a friendly manner. "Sure, there's a homeless problem. In any time of economic transition, there's bound to be some losers. A few people who happen to get sold into slavery or starve to death. It's tragic, I know. But for most people, things have never been better. The economy is booming, people are getting rich, and the markets are full of stuff most people hadn't even heard of ten years ago. So

what's all the fuss, li'l cuss?"

"A few dead widows and starving children may seem like a small price to pay so the rest of you can eat fresh grapes all year round, but let me tell you, wealth is temporary. The economy rises and it falls. Someday when the party comes to an end—and it always comes to an end—when our silky robes are in the pawn shop, and our strip malls are ghost towns, when that day comes, the only thing of value our people will have is the way we treat each other."

"Look," the king said, "I'm just going to lay it out for you. We're up to our balls in prophets. Israel needs a prophet about as much as literature needs another hundred Sweet Valley High novels. Thanks for coming by, though. You've given me a lot to think about."

The king then showed Amos to the door, and banished him from the country forever.

OBADIAH

TO THE PEOPLE OF Edom: You're flying pretty high now, but all things come to an end. Even an eagle dies in the mud.

Just in case you've forgotten, you are the descendants of Esau and we are the descendants of his brother, Jacob. Basically, we're cousins, and like good cousins, we are supposed to have each other's backs. But where were you when Israel was invaded? At harp lessons? Well, guess where we will be the next time you're up to your ass in Philistines? That's right. We'll be sitting on top of the hill, sipping our sweet wine and watching as your tents burn, your cattle are stolen, and your treasures are looted.

And there's no point in trying to prepare for the end, either.

"People of Edom, you're all a bunch of jerks!"

You're not going to know what hit you until it's too late. Your friends will betray you. Your attackers will come like thieves in the night. Only they won't be thieves, because thieves wouldn't take the time to beat you to death with rocks or salt the earth so it won't grow crops again. No, they'll be more like, I don't know, psychotic maniacs or something.

What's that? You're sorry? You want God to forgive you? Well, too bad! God doesn't want to hear any of it. There's nothing you can say to change his mind. You're dead men. You might as well break it to your kids that they're orphans. Or pre-orphans, to be more accurate. Say goodbye to your homes, your crops, and your little pre-orphan kids. Your day of reckoning is coming. And when it comes, Israel will be rebuilt, we will all be high and dry, and living the good life. No thanks to you, assholes.

Your Loving Cousin,
Obadiah the Prophet

JONAH

 OD WAS SICK TO THE teeth with Assyrians. They conquered Israel, looted its wealth, and scattered its people to the wind. Assyria was totally being a pill. So God sent a prophet named Jonah to their capital city, Nineveh, to tell the Assyrians that God was going to kill them all in forty days' time.

Jonah worried that they might not be entirely receptive to that idea. In fact, he worried that they might make balloon animals out of his testicles. So when he got to the docks, Jonah tried to give God the slip. Instead of going to Nineveh, he boarded a ship to the city of Tarshish.

But God is not easily fooled. He sent a storm to intercept Jonah's boat. Massive waves battered the ship, threatening to sink it. The storm was so bad that the sailors figured the supernatural might be at work. They drew straws to figure out who was to blame for the storm, and Jonah drew the short straw.

"What kind of god did you have to anger to cause a storm like *this*?" the sailors demanded to know.

"I'm a Jew," Jonah replied, "Our god created the ocean. Come to think of it, he also created the land."

"What is wrong with you? Why would you ruffle a god like that?" the sailors scolded. "What do we have to do to calm this god of yours down?"

"If you throw me overboard, everything will be fine," Jonah informed them.

As angry as they were with Jonah, throwing a passenger over the side of your ship wasn't really done, so the sailors persevered, bailing water and paddling for the shore. But when the storm worsened, and the whole ship seemed on the verge of sinking, they reluctantly tossed Jonah into the sea. The storm immediately stopped, the sun came out, and the ship sailed on its merry way.

Jonah, meanwhile, sank into the ocean and was swallowed whole by a giant fish. While trapped inside the intestinal tract of the fish, Jonah had time to take a moral inventory of his life.

"Why did I think I could cheat God?" he wondered. "For that matter, why should I be afraid of the Assyrians if God is on my side? If anyone so much as tickled me, God could have them swallowed

"Thanks for throwing me in the sea. Don't worry about it. God will take care of me."

by a fish, or beaten to death by an orangutan— or something."

It wasn't long before the fish lost its taste for minor prophets and vomited Jonah up onto the shore. Jonah, for his part, was no longer worried about what might happen to him. Smelling like a bucket of chum, he proudly marched into Nineveh. He wandered the city streets stinking of fish and telling everyone about the serious payback God was about to lay on them.

The Assyrians didn't try to kill him. They didn't even laugh at him. To his shock, the entire city fell flat on their faces and began praying for forgiveness. The king ordered everyone to roll around in the dirt and wear sackcloth as a sign of their humility. They even dressed their animals up in cute little sackcloth outfits.

"That's right," Jonah said, smug with power, "you should be afraid!"

Having delivered his message of doom, Jonah triumphantly marched out of the city, found a nice shady tree under which to sit, and waited for the fireworks to begin. Only the fireworks never came. God's deadline came and went and still Nineveh stood, every brick in place.

Jonah sat there, disappointed. "God, you told me you were going to destroy Nineveh. You brought me out here specifically to tell them that. I came hundreds of miles, INSIDE A FISH, goddammit! You're totally leaving me hanging, here."

"I changed my mind," God shrugged. "They were all so sad and apologetic. It made me feel sorry for them."

"Fine, but just so you know, I don't appreciate being made to look like an idiot."

God smote the shady tree Jonah was sitting under, causing it to whither, die, and topple over.

"Oh great!" Jonah said. "It's like a hundred degrees out here. Just kill me now. This is the worst day, ever."

"You're upset about the destruction of a single tree?" God said. "A tree you did nothing to plant, a tree you never watered, or nurtured in any way? That city over there has a hundred and twenty thousand people, every single one of whom I created and care about. Are you telling me their deaths shouldn't bother me?

"Just because they chose the wrong religion doesn't mean that I don't love them just as much as I love you."

MICAH

GOD IS COMING, and he doesn't look very happy. He's melting mountains and tearing up valleys, and if he catches you with some other god, something's going to get smashed. And when God gets all smashy, nobody wins. Samaria and Jerusalem will be reduced to rubble. Your children will be sold off as slaves. Your hair will fall out. Not a very nice vision of the future, is it?

Don't get me wrong, I'm not gloating. When this happens, it'll be the saddest day of my life. I'll cry like a jackal and moan like an owl. You can just imagine what that will sound like. I'll be so depressed that I'll walk around town naked for a few days.

I love our country, I really do. I just can't kid myself about the sort of things that are going on here anymore. We used to be a nation of people who treated each other like family, now the

"Hey sexy God, how about a date?"

rich and powerful are snatching up everything. The rest of us have no choice but to work their plantations or starve. If God wanted his people to be slaves, he would have left us laying bricks in Egypt. At least there we had cucumbers.

You know, it used to be that when you heard that your neighbor was in danger of losing their orchard, you would go over to lend a hand. Now, the only reason you stop by is to get a good deal on plums.

I realize that saying these things isn't going to make me a very popular man. But then, I'm not one of those prophets whose predictions get sweeter the more you put in his tip jar. If I wanted to be liked, I'd prophesy the coming of free wine. But I want you to know the truth of God's anger, even if you hate me for it.

Most of you seem to think that you can escape judgment so long as you ply God with sacrificial rams and olive oil. And maybe that's the problem— you simply think of God as one more public servant who needs to be bribed. But God doesn't need any more boar meat or lamp oil. In fact, there are only three things God wants from you. Are you listening? Here it is, the entire Jewish religion in a nutshell:

1. Build a just society where the rich and powerful don't get to treat the rest of us like livestock.

2. Don't get all too cool for school whenever God tries to tell you something. Be humble. You're never so holy that you can't improve a little.

And finally,

3. For gravy's sake, help each other out once in a while. Don't you understand? We're here on Earth to make life better for each other.

NAHUM

THE LORD'S NOT A hard guy, but don't fool yourselves, he will not let the nation that destroyed Israel go unpunished. You Assyrians think you're pretty hot corn, don't you? Well, let me tell you what's going to happen to your capital city: Nineveh will run dry. God will dry up all the wells, and your water will turn to sand. Your people will be parched. The cedars of Lebanon will wither.

Then, just for a dash of irony, he'll send in a flood to destroy you. Your idols will be smashed. Your children will all drown. Meanwhile, the people of Judah will celebrate your destruction with some extremely cool festivals and dances.

Then God will send soldiers dressed in red to plunder your city. Their chariots will buzz up and down your streets, and the soldiers will go door to door, looting your silver and gold and making your slaves moan like doves. Dead bodies will clog the gutters. This is what you've done to other nations, so now it's your turn. God is going to lift your skirt over your head and laugh at your naked body while he pelts you with shit.

You think your walls will keep you safe? You've destroyed walled cities before. You know that's not enough to keep you safe. The clouds are nothing but the dust God kicks up when he walks. Rocks shatter when he walks past. God is going to shake your fortresses like a tree and watch your soldiers fall out like loose figs.

And do you know what the worst part of all this will be? The fact that nobody's even going to miss you. When the world finally sees the Assyrians getting annihilated, people will cheer with joy. Maybe even do a backflip.

Welcome to NINEVEH HOME OF DRY WELLS, DEAD TREES, SMASHED IDOLS, AND DROWNED KIDS

HABAKKUK

Q: *Dear Lord, how long are you going to goddamn ignore me? Every day I pray for you to stop the Babylonians from killing us, and every day passes without you doing anything to help.*

A: Dear Habakkuk, why would I stop the Babylonians? I'm the one who sent them. I found the nastiest, least trustworthy people in the world, and raised them to become the totally bad-ass nation they are. Their horses are as fast as leopards and as mean as wolves. They laugh at fortified cities. They take prisoners like they're scooping up sand with a bucket. Their strength is their only god and their will is their only law. Totally bad-ass. They're going to run through you guys like bread through a goose.

Q: *Dear Lord, so you're using the Babylonians to punish us? Okay, I get that. But if you're going to punish us for being bad, doesn't it strike you as a tad unfair to use people who are ten times worse than we ever were? I mean, come on, that's like letting a serial killer pass sentence on a jaywalker.*

I was brought up to believe that you are a just god who rewards the righteous and punishes the wicked, but now I'm starting to think that's a crock of shit. Everywhere I look, I see prophets hiding for their lives while the corrupt rule. Have I been misinformed? Is justice simply not all that important to you? I eagerly await your reply.

A: Dear Habakkuk, who says I'm not going to punish the Babylonians, too? You're right, they're

"I don't feel very omnipotent today."

much worse than you are. They are idolatrous, blood-thirsty and as greedy as death. If they're the punishment for your sins, just imagine what kind of crazy shit I have in store for them. Don't worry, by the time I'm done, everybody will get the punishment they deserve.

Q: *No, no, you misunderstand. I'm not asking you to punish them, too. I'm asking you to ease up on all of us. To be honest, I'm not going to care if they're punished if I'm a severed head sitting on a pike somewhere. Sigh. Forget it. Look, I don't mean to tell you how to run your Universe, Lord. I guess you know what's best.*

You've done amazing things for us in the past, and I'm sure you will come through for us again. And there's certainly no question that you have the power to do whatever you want. If you wanted to, you could split a mountain in half. You could beat up a river. You could kill the moon with a spear. You're the greatest thing in the Universe and everyone everywhere should bow down to you as the Almighty God. But if I could just make one humble request of you before I go, it would be this: Don't rely entirely on your power to prove your greatness. Mercy can be an act of greatness, too. So if you could see your way clear to saving me from disembowelment, I sure would appreciate it.

"There goes Mr. Grumpy."

ZEPHANIAH

'LL KILL ANYTHING that moves," sayeth the Lord. "And those who survive will be living in shabby little mounds of rubble. I'll swat the birds right out of the sky. I'll beat up on fish for no good reason. That's how furious I am. The only reason I created human beings in the first place was so I could have some company, but since day one, I've been ignored, belittled, and jilted for hipster gods like Baal or Moloch.

"I'm saving my worst revenge for you, my 'Chosen People,' because you are always cheating on me. I'm going to run through the streets of Jerusalem at night with a lantern, so I can flat-blast you while you sleep. I'll dropkick your princes and smoke your merchants like cigarettes. I'll knock people out just for wearing foreign clothes. If you don't like it, ask Baal to save you.

"Don't think I'm joking, either. When I dish out my revenge, people will bleed like torn sandbags and shit out their entrails. You'll try to bribe me to make it stop, but guess what? I don't need your money!

"And it's not just the people of Israel who need to be worried, either. You'd better watch your ass, too, Philistines. You don't want me coming over for breakfast. And you Moabites have been talking a lot of smack lately. Ever hear of Sodom and Gomorrah? When I'm done, there will be nothing left of you but weeds and salt. Good luck convincing people to come live on your weed and salt farm!

"Don't laugh, Ethiopia. You're next on the list. And listen up, Assyria, because I am going to shake you up. Hard. When I am done with you there won't be a single owl left standing in a tree.

"Then I'll be sorry I hit you. I'll come around with flowers and try to take you out for brunch. I just don't understand why we have to keep going through all this. If you human beings would just be the friend I created you to be, I'd take care of you just like I did in the old days. I'd heal the sick and pamper the healthy. I'd massage the old and tickle babies. I guess I don't know what else to do. Maybe a few earthquakes and lightning attacks will get your attention. I just hope that when I'm done with all this killing, we can be cool. I really do want you to like me."

HAGGAI

FTER THIRTY YEARS IN exile, the Jews were back home in the Holy Land, rebuilding their houses, spackling their walls, and fixing their endtables. The prophet Haggai was troubled by the fact that, even as the nation was rebuilt, the Temple of Solomon still stood in ruins. He made it his personal mission to convince the people of Israel to return the Temple to its former glory.

"Listen, O Israel," said the prophet Haggai. "Now that the Lord has delivered you back unto the land of your fathers…"

"You mean Darius," someone interrupted.

"What's that?"

"It was the Emperor Darius who let us return to Israel."

"That's right," someone else chipped in. "I remember. It was all over the news."

"Ah," Haggai replied, "but who do you think made up Darius' mind to do so?"

"Darius."

"Okay let's call it a *joint* effort," Haggai conceded. "God and Darius have allowed you to return to Israel. The point is this: You've all been building your panel houses, and don't get me wrong, some of them are really cute, but now that we're back, thanks in some part to God, shouldn't we rebuild *his* house, too?

*"What the hell, guys?
Your break ended a decade ago."*

Remember that drought we had? I bet God would've spotted us some rain if we had asked him in his clean new Temple.

"Are there any old people here? You may remember what the old Temple looked like. Was it covered in rubble and rat shit? Is that the way you remember it? Me neither. You may also remember what a picky eater God was. If we tried bringing him a steak, and it touched his peas or his bread, we had to throw it out and start all over again. Does that sound like the kind of god you want eating in a pile of graffiti-covered ruins?"

Haggai turned to the governor, Zerubbabel, and said, "God told me that some day, very soon, he is going to conquer all the kingdoms of the Earth and rule the world himself from right here. From his Temple. And *you* can be the man who makes all that possible. Now, that's the sort of favor God doesn't forget."

Taking the hint, the governor immediately put construction crews to work, rebuilding the Temple.

"I can't tell you how happy I am at all the progress you've made rebuilding the Temple," Haggai told the governor. "And believe me, God notices. In fact, he told me that when he does come back to rule the world, you're going to be his right hand man. You're going to rule the world together."

"Really?"

"Oh, yes. Trust me, the day will come when everyone in the world will know the immortal name of Zerubbabel. But, for now, get back to work on the Temple."

ZECHARIAH

 I KNOW HAGGAI'S already gone over this with you, but we need to really to step it up on rebuilding the Temple. Let's set the whole reconstruction effort on rhumba beat and get it done as soon as possible, okay?

Once you get the Temple built, God will send us a Messiah— a leader who will free our nation of foreign rule. A king who will gather all the Jews scattered around the world, bring them home, and set up the Kingdom of God here on Earth. But God can only send the Messiah AFTER the Temple's finished. Don't ask me why, that's just what he told me.

And it's not enough to rebuild the Temple, either. You have to really be into it. You can't just fake-it-until-you-make-it the way you used to. God wants our obedience, but more than that, he wants a people who genuinely love him, and treat each other with respect. It doesn't work to sing inside the Temple and curse the widow begging on the steps. Because we didn't listen to him when he commanded us to be decent people, he didn't listen to us cry for help when we were getting stabbed to death by Babylonians.

In the old days, the Temple was a happy place, somewhere we could go to slay some goats and apologize to God. A healthy source of guilt and remorse, always there to remind us that we were being watched and shamed. And we need some shaming, to be frank. We need the Temple to inspire us to behave like God's chosen people, or he won't even bother with us. No Messiah, no Kingdom of God— nothing.

How do all I know this? Well, let me tell you about the dreams I've been having:

First, there was this flying scroll. It was like thirty feet long and it said that all the thieves and liars would be banished from the land. Then this angel appeared and said, "Come here, there's something I want to show you." He showed me a basket. He opened the lid, and there was a tiny woman trapped inside. "This is the sin of Israel," he said, slapping the basket lid shut before she could scramble out.

The angel disappeared with his scroll and his basket with the tiny woman and then the Lord himself appeared to me and said, "You have all sinned against me, but whatever, I just want to be together again. I want to go back to living in my Temple. I want to take care of you. I will make Jerusalem an unmovable rock, and when other nations attack you, I'll make their eyeballs rot out of their sockets and their tongues fall out of their mouths. I'll do the same to their horses, just to show you how much I love you.

"And when I come back, there'll be no more dicking around with emperors and kings, I'll just rule the entire planet myself. I won't just be the god of the Jews, but of the entire human race. And I will invite all the nations of the Earth to Jerusalem to celebrate the Feast of Tabernacles. Those who don't come won't get any rain for their crops while those who do will receive excellent gifts, including, but not limited to, free cookware."

Sounds great, doesn't it? But it all starts with getting the Temple rebuilt.

"I've got the banner...you've got the basket... are we forgetting anything?"

MALACHI

EOPLE OF JUDAH: This is God. First, I wanted to thank you for getting the Temple rebuilt and open for business. That said, I have a few things I need to go over with you.

After thirty years in exile, I knew you were bound to be a little rusty, but come on, priests. These are hands down the worst animal sacrifices I've ever had! A blind goat, really? Would you want to eat a blind goat? Or worse, that puking cow you sacrificed last week? Try taking the governor a cow that vomits every thirty seconds and see where that gets you. I'm sorry, but this meat is downright disgusting.

And it's not like you don't have plenty of nice, healthy animals to sacrifice. I see them running around all over the place. You're simply skimping on my sacrificial meat so you'll have more money to spend on shepherd staffs and robes, or whatever you kids are into these days.

I don't know what I've done to deserve such miserly contempt, but the next time some pagan empire comes storming through your country, enslaving your kids, and stealing your women, don't ask me for help. I'll be saving money on lightning bolts.

Oh, and do NOT try to cheese me out of my 10%. That's right, when you tithe, it's a full 10%. Maybe it will help if you don't think of tithing as an investment in my financial well-being so much as an investment in your own. You know those crops you plant? Well, you know who keeps them from being devoured by grasshoppers and mice every year? That would be me. So ask yourselves, do you want your crops to be looked after by a God who's fat and sassy? Or a God who's gassy from choking down epileptic sheep?

Am I making you nervous? Well, good! Because one day I'm going to judge each and every one of you according to your deeds. And my judgment will be like a crucible of fire, or a really strong laundry soap. Every stain, every impurity will be wiped out, and all that will be left will be honest, righteous men. Adulterers, liars, guys who bully widows, orphans, and immigrants, they will be set on fire, while the righteous will frolic like happy little rabbits.

"Is that all there is?"

THE NEW TESTAMENT

"Let me punch the address in my GPS."

"*Jesus? Jesus of Nazareth?
I haven't seen you since high school.*"

PART SIX
THE GOSPELS

The birth of Christianity. In which Jesus becomes a promising young street magician, the disciples dole out free health care, and people get nailed to stuff.

HE **JEWS HAD REBUILT THE TEMPLE OF SOLOMON, AS** instructed by God. Once the Temple was complete, they waited for God to make good on his promise by sending the Messiah, who would liberate them from foreign rule and set up the Kingdom of God on Earth. But hundreds of years passed and the Messiah never came. Meanwhile, Israel was passed around like a bucket of chicken from one empire to the next. The Persians took Israel from the Babylonians, and then handed them off to the Greeks, who were conquered by the Romans.

The Jews hated living under the Romans, and were sick of being second-class citizens in their own homeland. So every now and then, some brave soul would start a revolt, thinking maybe they were the Messiah the prophets had foretold. When King Herod died, one of his slaves, a tall, handsome man named Simon of Peraea, declared himself king. Israel had a long tradition of sexy rulers, so they figured, "Why not?" To which the Romans replied, "This is why not," and killed him.

Failed Messiahs would come and go. Someone would start talking big, they would lead a revolt, and the Romans would promptly squash them. Afterwards, they would crucify the aspiring Messiahs and plant them next to the road, where they would serve as human billboards, reminding travelers of what a good decision it was to remain loyal to the Roman Empire. The Jews began to wonder if the real Messiah was ever going to come, and if he did, could he avoid becoming a public service announcement?

It was into this world that a baby named Jesus would be born.

THE GOSPEL OF MATTHEW

ESUS WAS BORN IN A barn in a small town called Bethlehem. Despite his redneck beginnings, everyone seemed to realize that there was something really special about Jesus. Even foreigners noticed it.

Following an astrological sign auguring the birth of a new king, three wise men came to Israel to give Jesus some really expensive gifts, including gold, which was the ancient world's equivalent of a gift card, frankincense, which was a kind of perfume, and myrrh, which was almost the same thing as frankincense. The three wise men were not imaginative gift-givers.

Not everyone was happy to hear about the birth of this new king, though. The old king being one. When King Herod heard the prophecy that a new king had been born, he ordered his soldiers to kill everyone in Bethlehem under the age of two. Luckily, Jesus and his family managed to jump the border just in time. After living in Egypt as undocumented aliens for a couple of years, they returned home and settled in a small, out of the way town called Nazareth.

Jesus worked in the family carpentry shop, but when he turned thirty, he decided that what he really wanted to do was to travel the country and find himself, maybe do a little preaching. So Jesus began wandering from town to town, mostly talking to people about life, God, and love— though Jesus had an opinion on just about everything.

"When you give to the needy, do it because you're a decent, caring person, not because there's a crowd watching," Jesus said. "I see these guys in the market-place who make a big show of throwing coins to a blind man and I think, 'Shit, why not just bring a trumpet player with you?' If you need a fanfare every time you do something decent, then you're probably a miserable human being. It's when nobody's watching that God notices us most."

Jesus didn't have much use for people he thought to be pompous or pretentious.

"Don't be one of these holy roll-ers who launches into big, public prayers just to show everyone how religious they are. When people practice their religion in public, it's more for their benefit than it is for God's. As far as he's concerned, you might as well be praying in a cheese cellar.

"And don't get too hung up on material possessions. There's not one thing you own that can't be eaten, stolen or ruined. You should invest yourselves in the treasures no one can take from you."

Jesus also spent much of his time convincing people to drop out.

"The world is full of birds who've never had a real job, and yet they seem to get by all right," Jesus would say. "Work is an empty ritual to convince us that we're improving on nature. But it's a delusion. As big a dandy as he was, King Solomon never dressed half as good as a daisy.

"I guess I don't understand why we can't just accept the possibility that God actually wants us to like it here. When your son asks you to pass the fish, do you toss him a cobra? No? Then why are you so worried about what your heavenly father will pass on to you? We don't need to worry about starving to death. We just need to learn to ask God to pass the fish."

Jesus spoke a lot about God as a father. That's because God actually was his father. Jesus was a mixed-race child, the son of his human mother, Mary, and his father, God. One of the side effects of having God as his biological father was that Jesus possessed magical powers, which often proved useful.

He'd see a leper on the street and heal him, saying, "Okay, I'm going to heal you, but don't tell anybody, because I want people to focus on my teaching, not my magic tricks."

Of course, there's no way you keep something like that a secret. Tales of Jesus' miracles spread across the nation, and soon everyone was lining up so Jesus could heal them, or bring their dead kid back to life.

The demand for free health care was getting out of hand, so Jesus deputized twelve of his followers to be his official disciples. He granted the disciples magic powers to heal the sick and sent them on tour to heal people and spread his teachings.

"And don't charge anyone," Jesus warned them. "After all, I didn't charge you for your powers. In fact, don't bother with money at all. We'll just float from town to town and trust people to feed us and put us up for the night. I think you'll be surprised at how easy it is to live without money."

One man, hearing Jesus speak, stepped up and asked, "What do I need to do to enter the Kingdom of God?"

"Do you obey all the commandments?" Jesus asked. "You don't kill people or cheat on your wife, do you?"

"No, I obey all the commandments," he assured Jesus.

"That's great, you're halfway there!" Jesus said, clapping him on the back. "Now all you need to do is sell everything and come follow me!"

"Everything? I don't know, Jesus. I mean, my portfolio is really blowing up. I don't have a lot of liquidity right now…Hey, is that a two-headed goat?" When Jesus turned to look, the rich man beat it out of there.

"You see?" Jesus said to his disciples, laughing, "It is easier for a camel to squeeze through the eye of a needle than for a rich man to enter the Kingdom of God."

Jesus believed in an afterlife, which was a rather controversial thing for Jews to believe back then. He trained people to look beyond the material world, so they would be prepared to live as a spirit in Heaven after they died.

As Jesus described it, Hell is simply a place where the spirits of shallow people don't know what to do with themselves because there isn't a Pottery Barn.

One day, Jesus and his disciples climbed a mountain for a week-long spiritual retreat. Jesus went off by himself and it occurred to the disciples that nobody knew where he was. This bothered the disciple Peter, who sort of imagined himself to be second in charge.

"Great," Peter said, "We're only two days into our Radical Sabbatical and somebody's already gone missing."

Peter formed a search party, and when they finally found Jesus, they were stunned to find him in the middle of a conversation with the ghosts of Moses and the Prophet Elijah.

"Who exactly *are* you?" Peter asked.

"Who do you think I am?"

"I think you're the Messiah. And maybe not just the Messiah, maybe even the Son of God."

Jesus puppy-slapped Peter's cheek and said, "Well, don't tell anyone, okay? At least not yet. I'm not quite ready to reveal myself to the world."

People didn't do a very good job of keeping secrets back then, though. Once again, word got out about Jesus, and people started clamoring for this man who was supposed to be the Messiah. The people greeted him like a king and Jesus rode not one, but *two*, donkeys into the city of Jerusalem as people threw palm branches on the ground for his donkeys to walk on.

A group of aristocratic intellectuals called the Sadducees were annoyed by the fact that some uncouth hillbilly was getting the rock star treatment. They thought it would be fun to take Jesus down a peg and began pressing him on his belief in an afterlife, an idea which they found to be preposterous.

"So let's say a woman's husband dies and then she remarries. When they all come back to life in Heaven, whose wife is she?" one of them asked.

"Yeah, Jesus, answer that!"

"The fact that you would even ask that shows how little you understand," Jesus replied. "Nobody will be married in Heaven. In fact, they won't even really be people. They'll be, I don't know, like angels or something. But is that really your big argument? That Heaven can't be real because God couldn't figure out the paperwork?

"You are nothing but a bunch of self-righteous hypocrites! You talk to me about the word of God and the best you can do is try to nail me on a technicality? You have no love, no understanding, all you have is law. You follow God's laws while ignoring his commandments. You're like somebody who picks a dead fly out of a glass of water when there's a dead camel laying at the bottom of the well."

But winning his freestyle battle with the Sadducees came at a price. These men ran the Temple and the Sanhedrin, Jerusalem's religious court. Jesus had run afoul of powerful men, and he knew the jig was up. He took his disciples aside, and announced that he would soon be killed. One of the disciples, Judas, thought that if his religion was coming to an end anyway, he might as well cash in while he could. He went to the Sanhedrin and, in exchange for thirty pieces of silver, he agreed to lead them to Jesus so they could arrest him quietly.

Jesus thought it would be neat to have a big dinner party where he and the disciples could all be together one last time. He toasted his disciples, and lifting his glass of wine, he said, "Well, this is it, boys. Tonight, one of you is going to betray me. I will be arrested and put to death. This is the last glass of wine I'll ever drink until we all share one together in Heaven."

"What? Betray you?" they said. "Who is going to betray you?"

Jesus nodded at Judas.

"Oh shit...I just remembered, there's something I've got to do!"

Judas said, getting up and bolting out of the room.

After dinner, Jesus asked the remaining disciples to go pray with him outside in the garden, but it was getting late and the disciples fell asleep.

"Wake up!" Jesus growled. "Did you not hear me? I am a dead man. These are the last moments we'll ever spend together, and you'd rather have your beauty sleep?"

At this point, Judas reappeared. "Hey, I'm back! Anything happen while I was gone?" He walked up and kissed Jesus on the cheek, at which point dozens of armed men popped out from behind the trees and bushes, tackled Jesus, and tied him up.

"Whoa, who are those guys? They didn't come with me," Judas said unconvincingly.

The soldiers took Jesus to the Temple for interrogation. At this point, Judas began to have second thoughts about his silver parachute. He was haunted by the thought that he had betrayed his master. He tried to take the money back, but the Sanhedrin just sent him away. Disgusted with himself, Judas threw the money onto the floor of the Temple, found a nice

"Jesus, get back here right this second."

empty field, and hanged himself.

Meanwhile, the Sanhedrin would ask Jesus a question, and no matter what he said, they'd spit on him or kick him in the face. It was like he was stuck in a Japanese game show.

"We hear you think you are the Messiah, is that true? Are you here to save Israel from the Romans? Are you our king?"

"Well, yeah, but I'm more of an *alternative* king," Jesus replied. But they had heard enough.

Since Jesus claimed to be the Messiah, they sent him to the Roman governor so he could be executed for treason. The Romans flogged Jesus, tortured him, and made him carry his cross to the hill where they would crucify him. The soldiers thought it would be funny to dress him up in a purple robe and shove a crown made of sharp thorns down onto his head. They mockingly put a sign on his cross which read "King of the Jews." They nailed Jesus' hands and feet to the cross and hoisted him up, high atop the hill so everyone could laugh at him as he died.

Even the two guys who were being crucified along with him joined in the fun. "Hey, isn't that the guy who claimed to be the Son of God? Hey Junior," he shouted,

"how about getting us down? No? Okay, I just thought I'd check."

"You're such a dick!" the other one said, laughing. "If I could, I'd totally high-five you right now."

As if being made fun of by the entire world weren't bad enough, the soldiers who'd nailed him to the cross started gambling over his clothes and tried to make him drink vinegar out of a sponge.

As Jesus watched this circus unfold around him, on what had to have been the worst day of his life, he looked towards Heaven and cried, "My God! My God! Why have you forsaken me?!" And having said those words, he died.

When Jesus died, the sky went dark, the earth shook, and dead people all over town came back to life and started wandering through the city as zombies.

"Hey, maybe he *was* the Son of God, after all!" one of the soldiers mused.

They took Jesus' body and buried it in a tomb that had been donated by one of his fans. They sealed the tomb with a giant rock and posted a couple of guards outside to prevent his followers from stealing it. But that Sunday, there was a terrific earthquake. An angel came roaring down from Heaven and slid the rock out of the way, and the guards, who were never told their job would entail fighting angels, ran off in terror.

The next morning, some of Jesus' lady friends happened by and saw the angel, who was sitting on top of the rock, waiting for them. The angel told the women to go round up all the disciples, that Jesus was alive, and that he would meet up with them in the town of Galilee.

And sure enough, Jesus had come back to life, and was relaxing in Galilee.

"Jesus! I'm so glad you aren't, you know, dead. So, what's up next? Are we going back to Jerusalem? Should we perform a few miracles to get the ball rolling?"

"My work here is done," Jesus informed them. "I'm going back to Heaven to be with God. You're on your own."

"But…what are we supposed to do?" one of them asked.

"What do you mean?" Jesus replied. "You've just seen like three hundred miracles, including me coming back from the dead. Go tell people about it. Tell them I was the Son of God. Tell them the Messiah has come to get the world ready for the Kingdom of God. Oh, and tell them that I'll be coming back soon."

And with that, Jesus flew up to Heaven.

*"Are you here for the baptism?
Would you like a cricket?"*

THE GOSPEL OF MARK

 ARK'S TALE BEGINS with Jesus meeting John the Baptist, a mystic who lived in the desert and was so poor that he wore camel fur and ate crickets, which he made taste better by putting honey on them. John the Baptist got his name from the fact that he liked to baptize people, or dip them under water. A baptism was a bathing ritual which symbolized someone's rebirth as a spiritual being.

When Jesus was baptized, the skies parted and a dove fluttered down. In his booming voice, God announced to everybody that Jesus was his son, and boy was he proud of him.

Having gotten a big thumbs-up from God, Jesus went from town to town, doing God's work and dazzling people with miracles. He performed exorcisms, brought down fevers, and cured scores of lepers. Jesus had a thing for lepers.

Jesus was no snob. He would hang out with anybody. Soon, a cadre of fishermen, prostitutes, and other low-lifes began following him full time. He made twelve of these followers his official disciples. When asked how a supposed man of God could keep such sordid company, he merely shrugged and said, "Who needs a doctor more: the man who is well, or the man who is sick?"

While people loved his street magic, Jesus also started teaching his own religious philosophy, which rankled a lot of people.

"I like the free fish and bread," they'd complain, "But can't he just leave religion out of it?"

Jesus could not leave religion out of it. He went around telling people that all that really mattered was how much they loved God and how well they treated others, which especially bothered the Pharisees, who considered themselves to be holy men because they meticulously followed all the thousands of rules laid out by Moses.

"We're not about to let our life's work be undermined by some guy in homemade sandals," they vowed.

One day, the Pharisees caught Jesus picking grain in a field on the Sabbath, a clear violation of the Law of Moses. When they confronted him, Jesus shrugged them off, saying, "God made the Sabbath to serve man, not man to serve the Sabbath."

Meanwhile, Jesus' irreverent teachings and magic tricks were making him more and more controversial, and thus, more popular. As his following grew, Jesus decided to take his miracles up a notch. He was healing lepers and cripples by the busload. Eventually, he even began raising people from the dead. Jesus was making a lot of powerful people nervous, and they all began to think of ways they might quietly get rid of him.

But Jesus continued taking his show across the nation. One day, his tour took him by his old hometown. Everyone in this conservative sleepy town remembered him as little Jesus. Now he was coming back as this notorious shock preacher. His mother and his brothers worried that if Jesus started telling these people that he was the Son of God, or that they needed to follow him, he would get himself killed. They nervously tried to lead Jesus off the stage.

"Please, let us take him home," Mary begged. "He doesn't mean any harm, he's not right in the head."

"Yes, why don't you go home," the Pharisees argued. "Look, you're making your poor mother sick!"

But Jesus ignored his family, and the Pharisees, and launched into his routine, healing the sick and casting out demons. Seeing Jesus perform exorcisms, the Pharisees flipped out, accusing him of witchcraft and devil-worship.

"How does that make any sense at all?" Jesus asked them. "If I were working for the devil, wouldn't I be putting demons *in* people, rather than taking them *out?*"

Later, the Pharisees caught Jesus eating lunch without washing his hands first. They started in on him, blowing their whistles and shouting, "The Law of Moses requires you to wash your hands! You have defiled yourself, sir! You have eaten lunch without washing your hands, and now you are defiled!"

Jesus rolled his eyes, and said, "People aren't defiled half as much by what goes in their mouths as by the shit which comes out." Then he went back to eating his sandwich. The Pharisees decided they'd had just about enough of this smartass.

At one point during the tour, Jesus came upon a big commotion. His followers were arguing with a local family about whether they should ask Jesus to heal their son.

"What's going on here?" Jesus asked.

The father came over to Jesus and said, "It's my son. He's possessed by some seizure demon who causes him to flop around on the ground and foam at the mouth. The seizures get so bad that he'll flop right out of bed, or into the fireplace. Sometimes, when we're outdoors, he'll shake so hard that he rolls into the lake. We can't have him flopping into the lake. It's dangerous! I just don't know what to do anymore."

"How long has he been like that?" Jesus asked.

"All his life, I'm afraid."

Jesus walked over and put his hands on the boy. The boy shrieked and shook violently for a moment and then went limp and quiet.

"Oh my God, Jesus killed him!" someone cried out.

But after a few minutes, the boy came to, and everyone cheered.

"All the Pharisees do is scold and blow whistles at us," people said. "I'll take Jesus over those guys any day."

Jesus and his disciples stopped in Jerusalem for Passover. When he got to the Temple, he found the entrance lined with vendor booths selling animals for sacrifice and bankers exchanging money.

Jesus was enraged to find that the Temple had become more of a farmers market than a place of worship. He began knocking over the money-changing tables and horse-whipping the pigeon salesmen. This outburst put him in hot soup with the Sadducee priesthood who ran the Temple. They arrested Jesus and read a list of charges against him.

"God isn't interested in your laws," Jesus said. "He doesn't care about your sales figures. The only things God wants from you are the very things you lack: love and understanding."

"Jerusalem isn't some hayseed town," they explained to him. "Running amok and knocking over cash registers might be how things are done in East Nowhere, or wherever it is you come from, but here in Jerusalem, we have *laws*. We have a system. Put simply, you don't have any authority here. Now you're welcome to enjoy Passover, buy some souvenirs, whatever. Just don't forget who's in charge, okay, son?"

Jesus responded with a parable, "There was a vineyard."

"What, is he telling us a story, now?" one of the priests asked.

"Shhh! I want to hear this," another one said.

Jesus cleared his throat and continued. "The owner of the vineyard rented it to some nice, respectable-looking men, much like yourselves. Then, when the time came to harvest, the owner sent a servant to go collect the rent. Instead of paying up, though, the tenants beat the servant up and sent him away empty-handed.

'Hmmm, there must have been some mistake,' the owner thought, so he sent another servant, whom they killed. Finally, the owner said, 'I'll send my son, they wouldn't dare refuse to pay their due to my son.' But they killed him, too."

"What are you trying to say?" they asked him, annoyed.

"I'm saying that if you make the

"I have it all. Bread. Wine. Healing.
Raise the dead? No problem. Ask the whores
and lepers. Everyone is invited.
It's party time."

owner come back to the vineyard himself, there's probably going to be a change of management."

Whatever their faults, the priests had a firm grasp of subtext. Jesus was advocating revolution. This was the final straw, as far as they were concerned. And Jesus knew that it was only a matter of time before they came for him.

At first, they merely tried to ruin Jesus by tricking him into saying something stupid or that would get him arrested by the Romans. They asked Jesus whether he thought people ought to pay taxes, hoping that if he said "yes," he would lose his radical chic, or that if he said "no," he would be guilty of treason. Jesus slipped out of this rhetorical noose by brandishing a coin and asking whose face was on it. When the crowd answered that it was Caesar's, he simply told them that they should give Caesar that which already belongs to him. Then he shamed the priests by adding that they should pay God in what they owed him. The priests eventually gave up on trying to disgrace Jesus. They would simply arrest him, but they would tastefully wait until after Passover.

The day before Passover, Jesus decided to drop in on his friend, Simon the Leper. While he was sitting at the table, a woman cracked open an alabaster jar of expensive perfume and began pouring it over Jesus' hair.

"Ahhhhhh!" Jesus groaned in pleasure.

"What the hell do you think you're doing?" one of the other guests scolded her. "We can't afford that. That perfume was made out of pure nard!"

"I don't get it. What's the big deal?" Jesus asked.

"That perfume cost a lot of money," he explained. "We could have sold it and given the money to the poor."

"That was a really beautiful thing she did for me," Jesus replied, "and you just had to shit all over it. Look, you'll have plenty of time to take care of the poor, but I'm going to be dead soon, so just let me have this moment, all right? Geez." Jesus tied his sweet-smelling hair into a ponytail and carried on with his evening.

The next day, Jesus sent his disciples into town to make reservations for Passover dinner. After dinner, they were hanging out in a garden when one of their own sold Jesus out to the cops.

The cops took Jesus to the priests, who roughed him up, and asked if he thought he was the

Messiah. When Jesus replied that he was the Messiah, they sent him to the Roman governor, Pontius Pilate, to have him executed for treason.

The governor didn't think Jesus was much of a threat to the Roman Empire, so he invoked an ancient and poorly conceived custom that allowed a randomly assembled crowd pick a convict to be released from prison. He brought out Jesus and an insurgent named Barabbas and offered to free whichever one got the most applause from the crowd. The priests had stacked the crowd with their own people, so Barabbas was clearly the favorite.

"Are you sure you wouldn't rather have Jesus?" Pilate asked. "King of the Jews? Anybody?"

"No, the other one! Barabbas!" they shouted.

There was nothing left to do but have Jesus crucified. After Jesus died, they placed him in a tomb that had been donated by one of his friends and rolled a large stone against the door to seal off the entrance.

That Sunday, some ladies went to go visit Jesus' tomb. Among them were Jesus' mother, Mary, and his friend Mary Magdalene. They brought some perfume to rub on Jesus' corpse. "I think he would have liked that," Mary Magdalene said. "He liked to smell good."

They were walking to Jesus' tomb when his mother suddenly stopped.

"I can't believe I didn't think of this before," she said, "but how are we supposed to get inside? They rolled that giant rock in front of the door, remember?"

Nevertheless, they sallied forth with their perfume. When they arrived, the stone that had been sealing off the tomb had been rolled away.

Instead of Jesus' corpse, the women entered the tomb to find an angel in a white robe sitting on a bench.

"Where's Jesus?" they asked.

"Oh, he's running around here somewhere," the angel replied.

"You mean he's alive?"

"Well, sure," the angel replied. "You didn't honestly think they could kill a guy who brings the dead back to life, did you?"

THE GOSPEL OF LUKE

od decided that he wanted kids. So he talked a young woman named Mary into having his son. Perhaps more impressively, he convinced her fiancé Joseph that this was totally cool and nothing to worry about.

The couple were traveling to a small town named Bethlehem when Mary suddenly had to drop. Since the hotels were all full, God's son was born in a stable, among the cows, sheep and donkeys. Joseph and Mary named the baby Jesus.

Jesus was smart as a whip, and as you'd expect from a son of God's, he showed an early aptitude for religion. Joseph and Mary would take him to Jerusalem for Passover every year. One year, they were halfway home when they realized that Jesus wasn't with them. Nervously, they raced back to Jerusalem and searched everywhere, finally finding him in the Temple, debating the Torah with some priests.

"Jesus H. Christ!" his mother shouted, "Do you have any idea how worried we were about you?!"

"What's the big deal?" Jesus replied, "I was just visiting my father's house."

As an adult, Jesus decided to take up religion full time and became a traveling rabbi. He assembled a group of twelve disciples to be his assistants. They were a motley crew of fishermen, tax collectors, and failed revolutionaries. Jesus liked to give his disciples nicknames. He changed Simon's name to Peter, which means "rock." There was another Simon in his group whom he called "Zealot." He would refer to James and his brother John as "The Sons of Thunder."

Among the disciples who didn't get cool nicknames were Thomas, who was famous for being a skeptic (a rarity in someone who's joined a cult), and Judas, the guy who would later betray him. Being rather progressive for the times, Jesus also had several women in his inner circle, including Mary Magdalene, Mary of Bethany, and her sister Martha. Jesus and his disciples traveled all over Israel, telling stories, performing miracles, and freeloading at friends' houses. They were sort of like an improv group.

Jesus had a lot of ideas about religion. His most important

idea, though, was forgiveness. The ancient world in which he lived was all about revenge, killing, and constantly appeasing gods who would strike you with lightning just to watch you glow in the dark. Jesus thought, "Wouldn't life be nice if we all simply forgave each other? If I forgave you, I wouldn't feel the need for revenge. If you forgave me, I wouldn't need to be looking over my shoulder all the time. If God forgave all of us, we would see him more as a loving father than a cosmic policeman."

When the disciples asked Jesus how they should pray, he told them they should pray that God would forgive them as they forgave others.

"The old way is all about an eye for an eye and a tooth for a tooth," Jesus explained, "but I say if someone slaps you, offer him a shot at the other cheek. If he sues you for a coat, give him two. Why not? Sure, you'll be down two coats, but mentally speaking, you'll be able to move on. Let the other dude be consumed by guilt and pettiness for the rest of his life. Who needs it?"

Jesus didn't believe in revenge. "If the scales of justice need balancing out," he told people, "that's a job for God, not a lynch mob."

Jesus decided to go to Jerusalem. Some of the disciples went ahead to find a place to crash for the night at a nearby village of Samaritans.

"Well?" Jesus asked upon his disciples' return.

"They won't let us stop in their village," they replied. "Should we summon fire from Heaven to destroy their village, Lord?"

Jesus shook his head. "No, we're going to FORGIVE them. Have you heard nothing I've been talking about?"

Jesus' teachings greatly annoyed the religious establishment, especially the Pharisees. The Pharisees were a group of somewhat snobby holy men who prided themselves on being worthy of God's love by never breaking the rules. They made a point of following all God's laws, all the time, no matter how trivial they may be.

Jesus was having dinner at the house of a Pharisee named Simon. A woman showed up to the dinner uninvited. The woman had been ostracized because of some great sin she'd supposedly committed. Having nothing left to lose, she walked into the house, right past security, and went up to Jesus. Standing there face to face with him, unable to think of anything to do or say, she simply broke into tears.

In her grief and shame, her tears began to splatter onto Jesus' feet, so she bent down and began drying them with her hair.

"Will somebody get this skank out of here!" the Pharisee called out. But Jesus wouldn't send the woman away. "Can I ask you something, Simon?" Jesus asked.

"Sure," Simon replied, annoyed at the spectacle playing out on his dining room floor.

"There were these two people who owed a man some money. One of them owed him five hundred bucks, the other one only owed him fifty. Neither one had the money to pay him back, so he forgave both debts. Which of the two debtors do you think is going to be more grateful?"

"The one who owed him more, I suppose." Simon answered.

"And that is precisely why we should forgive those who sin the most." Jesus raised the woman up from her knees and wiped the tears from her eyes. "Go, and live in shame no more. Your sins are forgiven."

Jesus was always telling little stories like that. Most of his teachings came in the form of these little parables. Jesus liked to keep things simple. He once told a crowd of people that in order to be worthy of the Kingdom of God, they needed to do only two things: to love God and love their neighbor. Apparently, even that wasn't simple enough, as one guy immediately tried to lawyer-ball Jesus, asking him to define the term "neighbor."

"Is my neighbor the guy next door? The people on my street? My fellow Jews?" Predictably, Jesus responded with a story.

"A man was traveling when he was jumped by bandits who beat him up, robbed him, and left him for dead. He lay there bleeding on the street when a priest came riding by on a donkey. 'I'm saved!' the man thought, but the priest just trotted over him and kept on going.

"Later, someone else happened by— a man he recognized from his Synagogue. 'Okay, this time, I'm *really* saved!' the man reassured himself. But again, the traveler just puttered around him, taking care not to get any blood on his clothes.

"Finally, he saw a third man coming down the road, a Samaritan. We all know how much those Samaritans hate us Jews, right? Well, the poor man's laying there on the road thinking, 'Could this day get any shittier?' But the Samaritan stops, patches the man up, takes him to the nearest town, and sits by his bedside until he's healed.

He even pays the man's hospital bills. So, I'll put it to you…which one of those three men would you say was his neighbor?"

"It's the guy from the synagogue, right?" the man said confidently.

"Whatever," Jesus sighed.

Jesus saw adultery, murder, and materialism as the natural consequence of letting yourself be consumed with lust, hate, and greed. To Jesus, it didn't do you much good to constantly resist temptation. You suffer more from unrequited desires than the ones you actually give in to. And sooner or later, you'd probably act on those desires anyway, making all that self-denial meaningless torture.

The only solution, in Jesus' opinion, was to change your heart so you weren't full of terrible urges to begin with. To Jesus, it did as much damage to your soul to want to kill a man as it did to actually murder him.

All his talk about forgiveness and letting things go was a little too touchy-feely for the Pharisees. Jesus would be preaching to the multitudes while the Pharisees would gather in the back, grumbling to themselves, "What is this hippie bullshit?"

Jesus took his philosophy to Jerusalem. He was teaching in

The Last Call.

the Synagogue on the Sabbath, when he noticed an old woman with the worst case of osteoporosis he'd ever seen. She was hunched over like a human candy cane. So Jesus straightened her back, healing her. This really set the Pharisees off, who started berating Jesus for working on the Sabbath.

"You have six other days of the week on which to perform your miracles," they complained. "Come back on a Sunday! Anything wrong with healing somebody on a Sunday?"

"Do you think you can win God over with chores? You clean the graves of the prophets as an act of piety when it was the pious who killed the prophets in the first place. Maybe what God wants are more living, beating hearts and fewer undertakers."

Furious, one of the Pharisees took Jesus aside and told him that he should leave Jerusalem if he knew what was good for him.

"Why bother?" Jesus asked. "All the best prophets die in Jerusalem."

The Pharisees were impressed by Jesus' knowledge of the Torah, but they boiled with anger over his constant insults, and were appalled by the fact that he was trying to extend the love of God, which they'd earned through a lifetime of meticulous observance, to every

lush and pervert in the street.

"How can you possibly say that God loves these people who've spent their whole lives ignoring his commandments? How can somebody who despises the Laws of Moses ever become a Jew again?" the Pharisees wanted to know.

So Jesus told them the story of the Prodigal Son, which was about a spoiled rich kid who went on a drunken spending spree with his dad's money.

The Prodigal Son bugged his dad to get an advance on his inheritance. Once he got his hands on the money, he left his dad and brother on the farm, ran off to the city, and started living like a club kid. He bought expensive clothes, paid for his friends' drinks, and took them all out for barbecued goat every night. But it wasn't long before he ran through his daddy's money and found himself living on the streets. When the money was gone, all his party-friends disappeared. He was forced to beg for food and pawn his leather pants. His rock bottom moment came one day when he found himself picking leftover corn out of a pig trough.

Having blown through his inheritance, the Prodigal Son returned home in shame, hoping his dad would hire him on as a servant. He braced himself for how angry his dad would be. But when the father saw his emaciated, disheveled son trudging up the driveway, he ran out to meet him, wrapped a warm coat around his shoulders, and put a gold ring on his finger. That night he threw a party to celebrate the return of his lost son.

The man's other son didn't understand why his brother should get a party with balloons and cake for throwing his life away and wasting everything he had been given. The father turned to him and said, "Son, the fact that I love your brother doesn't mean I love you any less. You'll still get everything coming to you for leading a good life. But today, can't you just be happy that your brother has come back to us?"

Jesus was well aware of the enemies he'd made because of his teachings. Knowing that he was living on borrowed time, Jesus had one last Passover dinner with his disciples, where he announced that he was going to be killed soon. This caused an uproar among the disciples who, instead of saying, "Gee, that's too bad," or "We'll really miss you, Jesus," began arguing among themselves over who was going to take over when Jesus died.

So they asked Jesus to decide. "Lord, this is totally your call. Just tell us who'll be the boss when you're dead. Not that we want you to die, Lord. We're all very broken up about that. But is it me? It's me, isn't it?"

"You want to know which of you will lead after I'm gone?" Jesus asked.

"Yes!" they replied.

"Whichever one of you serves the most," Jesus said.

That night Jesus was arrested. They took him to the Roman governor, Pontius Pilate, on the grounds that Jesus was trying to lead a revolt and make himself king. Pilate found Jesus to be more pathetic than threatening, and didn't really want to deal with the whole mess, so he sent Jesus to King Herod and asked him to figure out whether or not Jesus was actually trying to put himself on the throne.

Herod was really excited to have Jesus at the palace, thinking he would put on a great magic show. To his disappointment, Herod found Jesus to be boring and something of a mope. So, as a joke, Herod dressed Jesus up in a king's robe and sent him back to Pilate. Seeing this skinny, sad man in a loincloth draped in a royal purple robe, Pilate bust out laughing. It was such a funny, mean-spirited joke that it instantly made Pilate and Herod best friends. He still wasn't convinced that Jesus was much of a threat, but wanting to keep everyone happy, Pilate relented and had Jesus executed, crucifying him on the outskirts of town.

As he slowly bled to death, it seemed like the whole world had gathered to ridicule Jesus. As he hung there dying, they beat and mocked Jesus for being so naive as to waste his time on pathetic and misguided ideas like forgiveness. For which he forgave them.

"What's up with all the planned obsolescence?"

THE GOSPEL OF JOHN

 IFE IN HEAVEN WAS a lonely affair, so God decided to shake things up by sending his spirit down to Earth to invite everyone to join him.

When his spirit floated down to Earth, it decided to inhabit a little baby named Jesus. You could even say that Jesus was the Son of God. When Jesus turned thirty years old, he put together a group of disciples, followers who worked as his assistants, bodyguards, and best friends. Together, they became regulars on the festival circuit, traveling all over Israel, and extending God's invitation to everyone they met.

Jesus and his disciples were just starting out when they were invited to a wedding. When the wedding reception ran out of wine, Jesus told the hosts to take their empty jugs out to the well and fill them with water. Once they'd done as they were told, Jesus transformed the water into wine. Everyone went on about how much better the magical wine was than the normal wine. The common practice in those days was to polish off the good wine at the beginning of the party and save the cheap stuff for later after everyone was too drunk to tell the difference, so having such good wine at the end of a party was a rare treat.

Every year, the Jews would all go to the Temple in Jerusalem to offer sacrifices to God and atone for their sins. The Temple was sort of like God's swear-jar. Before entering, visitors were required to cleanse themselves in a bathing ritual. As Jesus arrived, thousands of people were lined up outside the bathing pools, towels slung over their shoulder.

Everybody had broken at least one of Moses' laws, so everyone had to go. Moses had handed down so many laws that nobody could possibly follow them all. You could argue that the great genius of the Jewish religion was not in all its laws, but in the fact that you had to take a bath whenever you broke one.

People were also queued up outside the Temple, waiting to buy animals to sacrifice.

It was just another normal day at the Temple until Jesus showed up. But when he arrived, he was so irked by all the salesmen hawking subpar pigeons and sickly sheep that he began knocking over stalls and kicking over their cash baskets, which didn't go over too well with Temple management.

Jesus walked around Jerusalem, inviting everyone who would listen to join him in Heaven. Jesus explained that Heaven was like the most exclusive club they could imagine. But, luckily for them, he was the son of the owner, so he could put as many people on the guest list as he wanted.

Intrigued by Jesus' unorthodox theory that Heaven not only existed, but had a velvet rope, one of the priests, a man named Nicodemus, invited Jesus over for dinner.

"So how exactly does one get into Heaven?" he asked.

"You have to be born again," Jesus replied.

"You see, that might be a little tricky for me...I'm eighty-three years old."

"I'm speaking metaphorically," Jesus sighed, exasperated. "What I mean is that Heaven is a spiritual place, so in order to live there, you not only have to be born physically, but spiritually as well."

Jesus soon developed a large following. At one point, a crowd of five thousand people gathered to hear him talk. The sermon ran kind of long, and pretty soon it was dinnertime and nobody had brought anything to eat. Finally, the disciples turned up a boy who had had the foresight to bring five loaves of bread and two fish with him. Jesus took the food and started tearing it up, giving little chunks of bread and fish to the disciples to distribute to the crowd. Miraculously, no matter how much bread or fish Jesus tore off, he never ran out. He not only fed the entire multitude, but had leftovers, too.

"Well, I've seen enough!" someone said, finishing the last of his fish sandwich. "This guy is clearly the Messiah." The crowd cheered, and Jesus quietly slipped away before the mob could march him to Jerusalem, overthrow the government, and install him as king.

Since he was in the neighborhood, Jesus stopped by his hometown in Galilee. He told the people there, as he did everywhere, that he was the Son of God.

"I am the Bread of Life," he said. "Whoever eats my flesh will never be hungry again and will have everlasting life!"

"Well, that's a disturbing thought," someone said. "Did he really just advocate cannibalism?"

"Metaphors, people!" Jesus explained, "Metaphors! I have

come down from Heaven to bring you the amazing gift of eternal life. All you need to do is ask for it."

"You're not from Heaven," someone pointed out, "in fact, I know your parents, they live around here."

"Wait a minute…you mean that's little Jesus? Joseph and Mary's kid? I knew this was too good to be true." People began to leave.

"You don't understand," Jesus replied. "It's not Jesus who is feeding multitudes. It's not Jesus who is opening the gates of Heaven for you. It's the spirit of God living inside Jesus who is doing these things. Jesus is nothing more than a sack of skin, like you. If you were to let God live inside of you the way he lives in me, you could do these things, too. We can all become children of God."

"Yeah, whatever," they grumbled, walking away. "He had me going there for a minute."

Jesus and his disciples continued to plug away at the festival circuit, returning to Jerusalem for the Festival of Dedication. Jesus was at his booth in Solomon's colonnade, preaching and comparing himself to a good shepherd.

"A hired hand will run off the first time he sees a wolf or a lion. Those aren't his sheep, what does he care if they get devoured? But a shepherd who has invested his entire life in raising and taking care of these sheep? He will do whatever it takes to save them, even if it kills him…"

"Enough with the metaphors, already!" someone shouted. "No more 'Good Shepherds,' no more 'Bread of Life,' just tell us: are you the goddamn Messiah or not?"

"Yeah!" others called out, joining in.

"Ah, but if you were the Messiah's sheep," Jesus replied coyly, "you would know the sound of your shepherd's voice!"

"That's it, get him!" the mob grabbed stones and bricks to hurl at Jesus, who, slippery as always, got away just in time.

The people may have lacked patience for his esoteric imagery and the priests were constantly irritated at his blasphemous claim of being the Son of God, but everyone was amazed by Jesus' knowledge of the Torah and his miracles. The priests asked each other where the hell this guy had come from. Someone speculated that Jesus might be a prophet, but when they learned that he was from Galilee, they concluded that there was no way that God would ever send a prophet from a shit-hole like that.

"Water is fine, thanks."

Jesus was away when he heard that his good friend Lazarus had died. He came back to find Lazarus' sisters Mary and Martha beside themselves with grief.

"Don't worry," Jesus said, trying to comfort the sisters, "I can totally fix this. Really."

Lazarus had been dead for four days, so when they opened the door to Lazarus' tomb, the stench came billowing out like a cloud of smoke. Jesus fought his way past the stink and made his way into the darkened tomb. The crowd waited outside in hushed anticipation. Sure enough, after a few minutes, Jesus came walking out with Lazarus, alive and bandaged up like a mummy. The crowd went wild.

Jesus was having a celebratory dinner with Mary, Martha, and Lazarus. Mary broke open a pint of nard and poured it over Jesus' feet, wiping his feet dry with her hair and making the whole house smell sweet and lovely.

Judas objected to using such expensive perfume as foot cleaner. As the treasurer for Jesus and the disciples, he went on about how they could have sold the perfume and had enough money to feed the poor for another year, but the reality was that Judas was heavy into embezzlement and was disappointed that he wouldn't be able to dip his beak into Mary's nard.

When the priests caught wind of Lazarus' resurrection, they decided that something had to be done. If Jesus kept bringing people back to life, it wouldn't be long before everyone became a follower of his.

Jesus returned to Jerusalem for the Passover Festival. Everyone was abuzz about how Jesus brought Lazarus back to life. But despite this hero's welcome, Jesus knew he was walking into the wolf's lair and that it wouldn't be long before the authorities came to kill him. Jesus wanted to make his last night with the disciples count, so he threw a big Passover feast. During the dinner, Judas slipped away, ostensibly to get some more gefilte fish.

After dinner, Jesus and the disciples retired to a nearby olive grove. The disciples fell asleep, but Jesus, knowing that his arrest and death were imminent, said a prayer:

"Dear God, you sent your spirit down to inhabit this poor flesh, so that he might tell others about you and your Kingdom. Now my work is done and this flesh is about to die. And all I ask in return is that you look after his disciples once I'm gone," Jesus said, gesturing at the eleven men sprawled out on the grass, snoring. "I'm going to send them out into the world the same way you sent me out into the world. To be mocked, imprisoned, and killed so that their persecutors might join you in Heaven.

"They're like children, I know. They're selfish and loud and not all that bright, but they believe with such innocent intensity that it breaks my heart to think of the misery that awaits them. So could you cut them a break now and then? Maybe send the Holy Ghost to check in on them from time to time? He's not doing anything, anyway. That's all I ask. Be home soon. Got to go. Amen."

At this moment, Judas returned with soldiers to arrest Jesus. They took Jesus away, tried him, and sentenced him to death. That Friday, Jesus was crucified. As he hung there from the cross, dying, he looked up at Heaven and said, "It is finished."

"No, it's not," a soldier said. "You're still alive."

"Metaphors…" Jesus mumbled, "met…a…phors." And with that, Jesus died.

The crucifixion didn't really take, though, and three days later, Jesus was up and roaming around again.

After the crucifixion, life went somewhat back to normal for the disciples. Many of them went back to fishing. They were out in their boats, having a bad fishing day, when a kindly stranger yelled out from the shore that they should try throwing their fishing nets over the other side. When they did, they suddenly caught so many fish they could barely haul them into the boat. They immediately realized the stranger had to be Jesus, as he was always around when something really strange went down.

Jesus called the disciples to the shore and made them breakfast. Like he'd done years before, Jesus broke up the bread and divided the fish to feed his guests, but this time there were no fawning crowds, no fans hoping to see a miracle, just Jesus and his friends. Jesus asked Peter, "Do you love me?" "Of course!" Peter replied. "Do you love me, Simon?" "You know I do, Lord," said Simon. "Then feed my sheep," Jesus commanded them.

"But, you don't have any sheep…" Peter replied as Jesus vanished. "Well, that was weird."

"Oh, I think I get it!" Simon blurted out, "It was a metaphor! I think he wants us to take his teachings to everyone in the world who, in this allegory, are his sheep."

"Well then, why didn't he just *say* so?"

"Can I call you back?"

"If only I had some ink."

PART SEVEN
THE ACTS AND LETTERS OF PAUL

How to piss off friends and alienate strangers. In which many gentile converts nervously await the verdict on circumcision.

 T WAS EASY FOR PEOPLE TO LOVE JESUS CHRIST. HE TOLD great stories, he healed the sick, and chances were good that when he visited, he'd leave you with some free fish. Christ was easy. *Christianity* was a pain in the ass. First, there was the question of what exactly Christianity was. Was Judaism a gateway religion for Christianity? Or were Christians their own religion, completely separate from the Jews?

Furthermore, how do you convince people that Jesus Christ was the long-awaited Messiah, sent by God to liberate Israel from foreign rule, without someone pointing out that Jesus was dead and the place was still crawling with Romans? How do you convince pagans that Jesus isn't simply one more god they can throw onto the pile of gods they already worship?

Luckily, a guy named Paul came along who seemed to have answers to all these questions. In fact, lots of people, many of whom were more respected than Paul, had their own versions of Christianity, but Paul was smart enough to write his down. Kings may have money and power on their side, priests have tradition. But, in the end, writers always win. Kings die and traditions change, but nobody outlives a book.

THE BOOK OF ACTS

FTER JESUS CHRIST rose from the dead, his disciples couldn't wait to annoy the world with the good news.

Now, there is no better way to start a new religion than on a stomach full of waffles, so the disciples went out for breakfast.

They realized that if they were going to spread the word of Jesus Christ throughout the world, then they had a bit of a problem. They all came from the same place and spoke the same language. So how were they supposed to preach in other countries? As they argued amongst themselves, they started mumbling in strange words. The other diners in the restaurant thought they were drunk on syrup or something, but they weren't. They were speaking in tongues. God had sent The Holy Spirit, who was sort of the George Harrison of the Holy Trinity, to lend a hand. The Holy Spirit had given them all the ability to speak in foreign languages. So problem solved.

With their new foreign language skills, the disciples broke up into small groups and began traveling the world. Like Jesus, they popularized their message by performing magic tricks along the way.

At first, they focused on preaching to their fellow Jews. Peter and John went to Jerusalem. On their way into the city, they healed a crippled man who made his living begging by the city gate. Having use of his legs again for the first time in decades, the beggar started ed dancing behind them as they walked into the city. When the people of Jerusalem saw this guy who'd been crippled his whole life running and prancing around, they began to wonder if there might be something to this new religion.

The temple priests arrested Peter and John and discussed what to do next.

"I thought this whole Christian thing died out when Jesus was executed. Now we have to deal with this shit all over again?" one of them said, gesturing at the beggar who was still dancing outside the Temple.

"Well, those two guys definitely healed that beggar, there's no denying it," another one argued, "and we can't very well punish them for giving a man his legs back, so I think we should give them a pass on this one."

They brought Peter and John in before the court and announced their decision.

"Okay, we're going to let this one go. Consider this your warning cripple. Understand? But any more miracles like this one, or any more preaching about this Jesus guy, and the two of you go straight to jail. Got it?"

But the second Peter and John got back onto the streets, they ignored the warning and went right back to telling people about Jesus Christ, giving money to the poor, and healing the sick. Peter got so good at healing lepers that he would line them up in two rows and then cure them by running down the middle, high-fiving them along the way. The disciples were winning converts left and right, so the priests decided that a little tough love was in order.

They grabbed the next Christian they found, a guy named Stephen, and stoned him to death for blasphemy. When the crowd gathered to kill Stephen, a man named Saul volunteered to hold their coats.

"What a helpful young man!" they said as they handed Saul their wool coats, "I wish more kids today were like you."

"Have fun at the stoning!" Saul waved.

When the disciples heard about Stephen's death, they scattered in fear. Some went to Samaria, some went to Gaza, others set up shop in Damascus.

Despite being on the run, Peter, John and the rest of the disciples continued preaching and performing miracles. The priests in Jerusalem soon realized that snuffing out this new cult was going to take a little more elbow grease than just stoning one guy, so after he returned everyone's coats, they enlisted Saul to track down and arrest Christians when and where he could find them.

Saul was traveling to the city of Damascus when he was blinded by an intense light. Then a loud, booming voice bellowed from the sky.

"Saul! Saul! What the hell, man?"

"Please," Saul asked timidly, "who are you and why did you blind me?"

"This is Jesus Christ! Yes, *that* Jesus Christ! You think you're doing God's work? You are killing the people I sent to prepare the world for God's Kingdom. Not the best way to get on God's good side, Saul! Now, go into town and await

further instructions. I'm very disappointed in you, Saul!"

Saul stumbled blindly into
town, where a local Christian took
him and cared for him until his
eyesight returned. Saul converted
to Christianity and spent a couple
of months learning about his new
religion from Peter and James.

Nobody matches the zeal of a
new convert, or gets as much done
as someone who doesn't know
what they're doing. Saul had both
those things going for him. After
his crash course in Christianity,
Saul made it his mission to convert
pagans to his faith.

He changed his name to Paul,
which he felt was less Jewy.
The rechristened Paul was released
into the streets of Damascus like a
pit bull, performing miracles, telling everyone about Jesus, making
fun of their religions, and generally
riling people up. He became so
unpopular that the other Christians had to hide him in a basket
and lower him over the city wall
at night, just so he could get out of
Damascus alive.

Having escaped Damascus, Paul
traveled to Antioch, where he told
the locals that if they believed in
the resurrection of Jesus Christ,

*"Can I hold your coats while you
stone the heathen?"*

not only would Jesus forgive them of every rotten thing they'd ever done, but he would give them everlasting life, too. That seemed like a pretty good deal to the Gentiles, and Paul won many converts. But when he tried to preach in the synagogues, his fellow Jews were a little put off.

"We already know about God," they said dismissively. "And who is this Jesus character, anyway? What chutzpah to think that he can forgive my sins!"

Some of the Christians who'd stayed behind in Jerusalem came out to Antioch to meet all these new Gentile Christian converts Paul had made. "Wow, so all you Gentiles are Christians, now?" they asked, impressed. The men nodded. "Really? You've all been circumcised and everything?"

"What?" the men asked, smiling nervously.

"Well, of course, you've got to get circumcised. You've got to become a Jew in order to convert to Christianity. Christianity is a Jewish religion, after all."

This bit of fine print caused something of a furor in the Christian community. The disciples and the other church leaders held a conference in Jerusalem to discuss whether grown men had to get their foreskin lopped off in order to become Christians.

After much wrangling and debate, they arrived at a fateful decision. They immediately sent an urgent letter to the Gentile Christians in Antioch letting them know that no, they did not have to get circumcised, but that they shouldn't interpret this as an open door policy for all the other pagan stuff they used to do. They could not, for instance, worship idols, monkey around with prostitutes, or eat anything which had been strangled to death. But, as far as circumcision went, they could keep their little pagan dongs intact.

With the circumcision matter settled, Paul continued on to the city of Philippi. He was on his way to a prayer meeting when he encountered a young oracle telling people their futures.

"Hmm," Paul said, stroking his chin, "Poor girl appears to be possessed by demons." Paul walked up behind her and performed a quick exorcism. Satisfied in having done his good deed for the day, Paul was surprised to find himself being arrested. His exorcism had taken away the oracle's ability to see the future, thus robbing her of her livelihood. Now she wanted to press charges.

The cops roughed Paul up and threw him into a dingy, rat-infested cell. They would have left him there to rot, but Paul happened to mention that he was a Roman citizen. When you were running a Roman puppet state, beating up and detaining Roman citizens without a trial wasn't a winning strategy. So the jailor and the city elders dusted Paul off, let him out of jail, and walked him to the gate, hoping that he would see this incident as a funny mistake, something they could all laugh about later.

Paul left Philippi and traveled the world, preaching the word and angering many diverse people in exotic locales.

In Ephesus, Paul told the crowds that as gratifying as it may be to worship a ten-breasted woman, Artemis was, nonetheless, a false god. Which would be a little like standing outside Disneyland and accusing Mickey Mouse of being a child molester, as the whole town made its living working at the Temple of Artemis, or selling little silver action figures of the goddess. There was a riot, and the whole town came out to defend Artemis, adding Ephesus to the long list of places Paul barely escaped alive.

In Jerusalem, Paul went to the Temple to pray. When the locals recognized him, they went berserk. Here was the turncoat whom they'd sent out to knock some sense into the Christians, who instead went into every synagogue in the world to convert Jews to Christianity, convincing them to turn their backs on the Law of Moses. A mob formed and dragged Paul out of the Temple. They handed their coats to another nice young man and prepared to stone Paul to death, just as they had done to Stephen.

Luckily for him, a couple of Roman soldiers noticed the commotion. They handcuffed Paul and made him sit on the curb until they could get to the bottom of things.

"Okay, what seems to be the trouble here?" the soldiers asked.

Everyone in the crowd started shouting over each other, demanding Paul's death.

Addressing the crowd, the soldier said, "Now come on, you know I can't kill him. But would it make you feel better if I flogged him a little bit?"

At this point, Paul once again played his trump card. "You can't flog me," he said, "I'm a Roman citizen! I have rights!"

"You're a Roman citizen?" the soldier asked, to which Paul nodded.

"Shit. Looks like we've got to take this one downtown."

So the soldiers carted Paul off to Caesarea to await trial. The way the Roman legal system worked, if you wanted your trial to come up on the docket anytime soon, you needed to lubricate the wheels of justice with a few well-placed bribes. Paul apparently didn't know this, or he refused to take part in this particular nuance of Roman law. After a couple of years in jail, Paul got sick of waiting for his trial and appealed directly to have his case heard by the Emperor of Rome, which was his right as a Roman citizen.

Soon after filing his appeal, as fate would have it, Paul was finally summoned before the governor for his long-awaited trial.

"What's he accused of?" the governor asked.

"He worships some dead guy who he says came back to life and is now a god," the clerk said.

"How the hell am I supposed to investigate something like *that?!*" Turning to Paul, he said, "Okay, what do you have to say for yourself?"

Paul told the governor all about how he was blinded on the way to Damascus, and about how Jesus had appeared to him in a vision and gave him the power to heal people, and about all his misadventures and narrow escapes telling people about Jesus.

"Guess what? God came to me in a dream and told me that it's cool to eat bacon."

"Well, Paul, that's about as crazy as a story I've ever heard, but there's no law against crazy, so I suppose you're free to go."

As the governor rifled through the paperwork to sign Paul's release, he came across Paul's appeal to Rome. "What's this? It says here that you've already petitioned to have your case heard by the Emperor. Why'd you go and do a silly thing like that? Now I can't release you. I have to send you to Rome to stand trial."

"That's okay," Paul said, "I wanted to go to Rome, anyway. And that Nero seems like a reasonable young man. I'm sure I'll be just fine."

Paul was never heard from again. That is to say, he never left Rome alive. He spent the rest of his life in jail, which gave him plenty of time to write letters. Until the day he died, he would continue annoying people for Christ, if only through the mail.

"Can you cure my hangover?"

PAUL'S LETTER TO THE ROMANS

 EAR ROMANS,

Okay, apparently I got some hecklers out there, some wise apples who feel qualified to question my teachings. I don't suppose any of them were blinded on the way to Damascus, or had Jesus personally appear to them in a vision, but whatever.

First off, allow me to make this clear: Christianity is for everybody. I realize most of you are Jews from the old country, but that doesn't mean you get to look down on the pagan newbies. In fact, if anything, you should admire them— they have enough faith to accept Jesus Christ without knowing anything about God or the prophets. So mad props to our Roman friends.

What's more, just because you were born Jews, that doesn't mean you get to moonwalk into Heaven just by following the Laws of Moses. The Roman Empire has laws, too. Not breaking them doesn't make you a holy man, it just makes you someone who doesn't like being nailed to wooden objects.

So it is with God's laws. Look, your soul is like a snarling dog. The Laws of Moses won't tame or change your soul,

"Are you sure you wouldn't rather take Jesus into your heart?"

they merely provide a cage to contain it. But salvation is not about staying inside a cage. It's about transforming your soul so you don't need a cage to begin with. It's your soul which will live on in Heaven, not the cage. Do you think God wants thousands of feral dogs running loose in Heaven, chewing up the furniture? He does not. He wants your soul to grow, mature, and transform itself into something worthy of Heaven.

On the other hand, just because your salvation does not come from following the law, that doesn't mean you get to go buck wild on Earth, either. I know the expression goes "that when in Rome…" but I really wish you wouldn't take that so literally. Especially when it comes to orgies. Let's face it, Rome is full of deceitful, idol-worshiping, effeminate drunks and whores (present company excepted, of course). The less you learn from them the better.

I'm not saying you should look down on your fellow Romans. The whole point of Christianity is to let sinners find forgiveness. Just that you should be the ones rubbing off on them, not the other way around. And really, it shouldn't be that hard to win them over.

In other religions, you have to bathe in cow blood or cripple yourself crawling to a shrine to get absolution. For us, all we have to do is admit we were wrong and believe in Jesus Christ. Our religion is much more efficient, and way easier on the knees. But we have to stop thinking of ourselves as a side gig for Jews. We're our own religion now, open to everybody. Everyone needs God, not just Jews.

While it's easy to become a Christian, living like a Christian can be tricky and difficult, like giving a turtle a massage. Especially since life is so full of fun and temptation.

So maybe, as Christians, it's simply better that you think of yourselves as dead people. The law, hunger, fear, lust: none of these things apply to the dead. So think of yourself as dead people and act accordingly. Preach the gospel as if you have no fear of being arrested, live as if you don't need to sin, and love each other as if you have no fear of being betrayed. It's kind of liberating being dead, isn't it?

My congratulations on your recent death,
Paul

PAUL'S 1ST LETTER TO THE CORINTHIANS

 EAR CORINTHIANS,
I hear you guys are having trouble keeping it together. A lot of you are forming factions, wasting your time arguing over scriptural minutiae, and trying to one-up each other with clever arguments. Knock it off. Trying to top each other like this is pointless. It's just a game of intellectual gin rummy designed to show off how smart you are. It does nothing to bring you closer to God.

Do you think God is impressed by your wisdom? Are you impressed by a cockroach who figures out how to crawl into your sock? We are all mere insects compared to God. Besides, I hate to break this to you, but we're not exactly converting people by the power of our intellectual arguments. I've won more converts than the rest of you combined, and I'm a homeless guy in a wool skirt.

Let's be honest: what we are asking people to believe doesn't make a whole lot of sense. All we can really do is tell them about Christ and hope they bite. Either the stories about his miracles and coming back from the dead work for them, or they think we're crazy. That's it. In the end, God does not call us to be debaters or professors or philosophers. He calls upon us to be fools for Christ.

This makes it hard to preach the gospel, I know. Jews always want proof, Greeks love a persuasive argument, and we don't have much of either. But then, I didn't come to Corinth armed with anything more than my story and you all fell for it. So don't lose heart. Just speak your truth and see what happens.

By the way, I've been told that some of you former pagans aren't ready to buy into the whole Judeo-Christian morality thing, yet. I even heard that one of you is having an affair with his father's wife. Again, knock it off.

I know I've been telling everyone they don't need to follow the Laws of Moses anymore, so the timing of this is somewhat awkward, but while that's true, there are *some* rules I really need to insist you start following:

1. All this extra-marital sex has got to stop. In fact, I'd prefer you not to have any sex at all and focus that energy on serving God. But if you absolutely, positively got to do it, you should get married and then just have the sex with that one person.

2. Don't eat meat that's been sacrificed to idols, even if it means you have to become a vegetarian.

3. Women must cover their heads when they pray. Last time I was in your church I saw a bunch of women praying without any kind of head covering whatsoever and it just looked, I don't know, weird.

4. Men, on the other hand, may NOT cover their heads in church. That's just the way it is.

5. Also, men, don't try to score extra money working as male prostitutes. Nor should you patronize prostitutes, male or not. I don't care if you're playing pitcher or catcher. Every time a prostitute is paid, chances are that some of that money is going to a pagan temple. So don't support the competition.

6. Speaking in tongues is cool, but make sure it's really God that's speaking through you. Don't fake it.

7. When you celebrate the Lord's Supper, or have a love feast, it needs to be a potluck and not a brown bag. Last time I was there, everyone brought their own food, and there was some asshole getting drunk on wine and gorging himself with roast lamb, while all the guy next to him had to munch on were a few crackers. Do you have any idea how bad this looks? If you want to keep your fancy snacks to yourself, eat at home. When we eat together, we should share everything, like family. What good does it do to celebrate our brotherhood by embarrassing the guy sitting next to you?

Remember, I love you all like family and I only want what's best for you. I'm sorry if it feels like I'm guilt-tripping you or making you feel bad about yourselves. But then again, the purpose of religion, like family, is to make us feel loved and inadequate all at the same time.

"You're having an affair with your father's wife...Can you tell me about that?"

If you could only remember one rule that I give you, it would be this: speak and act towards each other with love. You could be the best dude in the world, your words could be as sweet as angel's piss, but if there's no love in them, you're just a clanging cymbal. Love doesn't try to pin someone down in an argument or make you feel better than others. Love doesn't get angry or keep score. Love is being patient with people, letting them up when they've been knocked down. You could do everything else right, but if you don't act with love, it's all camel shit in the end.

Love,
Paul

P.S. Be sure to pass the collection plate at the beginning of the week when people have money rather than at the end of the week, when everyone's broke. I know this is difficult seeing as how you have your services on Saturday and all, but it's important to hit people up when they've actually got the cash. If need be, we can always move our church services to Sunday.

PAUL'S 2ND LETTER TO THE CORINTHIANS

 EAR CORINTHIANS, Sorry I haven't been able to come to Corinth for a visit, but things have been going kind of crummy for me here in Asia. I'm afraid if I showed up I'd just be a downer.

I heard you finally took care of that guy who was sleeping with his dad's wife. Good! Though, as long as he's sorry and he's promised to stop, you should ease up and let him back in the church. Remember, forgiveness is kind of the whole reason we're all Christians in the first place. While the laws of men can only really offer punishment as motivation, Christ is more about rewarding faith than he is about punishing sin. So we're basically carrot people by nature, not stick people.

Again, I'm sorry if I came across a little gruff in my last letter. You've got a fabulous church going there, and Titus has nothing but praise for you people. But don't get cocky. I've heard that you've been giving letters of recommendation to people in your church to show when they go out to preach. Do you have any idea how pretentious that sounds? When spreading the love of Christ, you're not supposed to be handing out letters of recommendation, you're supposed to BE the letter of recommendation. Acting with love and forgiveness is way more convincing to people than handing them your résumé.

It's also come to my attention that some of you are afraid to go out and preach the word of God. Something about not wanting to get whipped, beaten, or crucified?

Here's a little thought experiment which will help you get past your fear: think of your soul as someone who's camping and your body as a really shitty tent. Your tent is drafty and cold, it leaks, and your soul barely fits inside. Eventually, if all goes right, your tent will get old and collapse. Luckily, our tents are encamped right outside God's castle. So don't worry if barbarians come and stomp your tent into the ground. If that happens, God will let you

"We're about carrots, not sticks."

move into his nice warm castle. Upgrade!

Also, as you know, the church in Jerusalem is dead broke. Could you throw them a few shekels? In future, it would be nice if I didn't even have to ask. You should just take the initiative and help your fellow Christians from time to time.

By the way, I've heard that some pompous blowhards have been teaching you some rather questionable things. Some of them have even taken to describing themselves as "super-apostles." How freaking lame is that! What, do they have the power of laser-prayer?

But what really burns me up is when I hear about these haters talking smack about me, saying that I don't know dick about the word of God. When this happens, would it kill you to speak up for me? If I stand up for myself, then they accuse me of tooting my own horn. But then if I let them belittle me and say nothing in my own defense, it only encourages them. It would be nice to know that you've got my back. That's all I'm saying.

Love in Christ,
Paul

P.S. I'll be sending Titus by to pick up your donations. Don't make me look like an asshole, people.

PAUL'S LETTER TO THE GALATIANS

EAR GALATIANS,
I can't believe my freaking ears. I leave you alone for one minute and already you've abandoned everything I've taught you and are trying to live like Jews again? I don't care who told you that you have to eat kosher and get circumcised in order to be a Christian. I don't care if James or Peter say that I am "unqualified" to teach you. My gospel comes straight from Jesus Christ, who appeared to me in a vision, blinded me, and told me to spread his word. Not a four-year degree in Jesus Studies, I'll admit, but pretty darn good as qualifications go.

I'll level with you. I used to be a pretty hardcore Jew. In fact, I was a fundamentalist. In fact, I used to kill Christians for blasphemy. But my vision of Jesus Christ changed me. It made me realize that we were all God's people.

Speaking of Peter, I totally had it out with him the other day over this very thing. When we were together in Antioch, he was as happy as a dog in gravy to be eating with the Gentile Christians.

Totally violating the Laws of Moses, of course, but no big deal, right? But then when some of James' followers showed up from the old neighborhood, suddenly he became Mister Kosher. Too good to even sit with the Gentiles.

I came in and all the circumcised dudes were lined up on one side of the room while all the uncut guys were lined up on the other. Nobody was mingling. The whole place looked like an eighth grade dance. So I called Peter out in front of everybody.

"Peter," I said, "just last week we were eating pork cutlets together and now you don't even want to sit next to a guy just because he's uncircumcised? I thought we were all brothers here!"

Besides, I don't know what they're moaning about. I'd already cleared my teachings with James and Peter and all the church leaders in Jerusalem. I even brought Titus along so they could see an uncircumcised Christian for themselves, and they totally lapped him up! They went on and on about how well-behaved he was, so I don't know what their problem is.

So for the last time: you do NOT have to get circumcised to be a Christian. Okay? Hopefully this letter will come in time to stop anyone who's signed up for the operation. You don't earn salvation like you earn a merit badge. No amount of circumcisions will bring you closer to God if you don't have faith in him.

Anyone remember Abraham? The patriarch of the Jewish people? The Laws of Moses weren't written until hundreds of years after Abraham's death, but God still chose Abraham as his best friend and the father of our nation. Clearly, what attracted God to Abraham wasn't his circumcised penis, or the fact that he never ate pheasant or trimmed his beard.

Abraham never even heard of those laws. What made Abraham worthwhile to God was his faith.

Abraham, if you'll remember, had two sons: Ishmael and Isaac. Ishmael was born to a slave, was treated like a piece of property, and was a son in name only. Isaac was born to Abraham's wife, he treated Abraham like a father and Abraham loved him like a son.

As the descendants of Abraham, we need to ask ourselves: What kind of son do we want to be? Slaves to the law who never get to really be close to our father? Or the son who gets to go out and play grab-ass, who loves his father and is loved by him? All the Law offers us is the life of Ishmael. Our faith gives us the chance to be Isaac.

"I just got a note from Paul — 'Never mind about the circumcision.'"

Look, all I've ever wanted to do was to make God happy. If I still thought that following the Laws of Moses were what God really wanted of me, I wouldn't even bother being a Christian. I'd still be a Jew. I'd still be a fundamentalist.

In fact, I'd be on my way to kill you all right now.

Anyway, I hope this clears things up. Don't make me come down there.

Hugs and Kisses,
Paul

PAUL'S LETTER TO THE EPHESIANS

 O THE CHURCH OF Ephesus:
Isn't it great to be a Christian? You used to be a bunch of crazy pagans, running around, jumping on the furniture, having sex with whoever you wanted. But thanks to the power of Jesus Christ, you've been transformed into new, fulfilling lives, full of self-denial and persecution.

You're so civilized now that I don't even think of you as savages anymore. Some people still make a big deal over the fact that you guys haven't been circumcised, but I don't care. It doesn't matter that some of us were born Jews and others were born Gentiles, all that matters is that we're one people under God. So keep your dicks just the way you like them.

While I don't care if you're hung like pagans, I really must insist that you stop thinking like pagans. You know what I mean. The dishonesty. The violence. The temper tantrums. Remember, becoming Christians was supposed to make new people out of you. So here's a little advice: Don't let the sun go down on you while you're still angry. Don't let a grudge ruin the fudge, people.

If you've been stealing other people's shit, give it back. And for Christ's sake, don't tell dirty jokes or gossip about each other. That sort of thing just devours a church from the inside out. You need to forgive each other, just as Christ forgave you.

Some of you aren't going to want to hear this, but here it goes:

"All I'm saying is, if you're going to be a slave, be a good slave."

ladies, you need to submit to your husbands. That goes for you, too, slaves. Don't be getting all uppity. Obey your master as if you were taking orders from Christ himself. Not that Christ would own slaves.

On the flip side, if you do own slaves, treat them well. Remember, you both serve the same master in Heaven, and he's way too powerful to care which one of you is the slave and which one is the master here on Earth. That'd be like you trying to figure out which one of the flies buzzing around your head was in charge of the other. And

men, just because you're the head of the family and your wife has to do whatever you tell her to, that doesn't mean you get to be an uncaring, emotionally unavailable jerk. Make her happy she married you.

Anyway, follow my advice and remember to pray for each other and everything will be okay. Oh, and you might say a few prayers for me, too. As it happens, I'm in jail again.

Smooches!
Paul

PAUL'S LETTER TO THE PHILIPPIANS

DEAR **P**HILIPPIANS,
You know, on the whole, I think my imprisonment has actually been an asset to our cause. Aside from the fact that it's given me the chance to share our beliefs with my guards (some of whom are actually quite nice!), you all have really responded by picking up the slack and preaching in my absence. Some of you are genuinely trying to win converts.

Others are out there preaching because you see an opportunity to move up the church ladder now that I'm out of the picture. And frankly, I don't care what your motives are, as long as you're out there preaching.

If your ambition is to make it to the top, though, then I have to say you are really missing the point of what our whole movement is about. We worship a guy who, even though he was God,

"Signed, Sexy at Sixty."

decided to take human form just so he could die for the human race. So the pinnacle of Christian achievement isn't to become a king, it's to become a martyr.

It's a strange notion for humans to wrap their heads around, I know, but don't get confused by the critics. They'll try to tempt you, out-talk you and make you feel stupid for turning your back on the good life. But their destiny is the grave, their god is their stomach, and their legacy will be whatever perversions they managed to get away with during their lifetimes. Your destiny, on the other hand, is eternal life, your god is the Almighty, and your legacy is all the people you've served. So there.

Stay focused. If you're going to criticize people for being loose and immoral, then you need to be able to resist temptation yourself, or you're going to end up looking like a total douche. If you want to be a star, then you've really got to shine.

By the way, before I forget, I wanted to say thank you for the AWESOME care package! You Philippians really know how to make a guy feel special! You always have. I remember the early days, when I was traveling through Greece, spreading the gospel. While none of the other churches would give me the ass-end of a pretzel, you guys took me in, fed me, and treated me like one of your own. I will never forget that.

Oh, and thanks for sending me Epaphroditus to help me with my work. Unfortunately, I'm sending him back, because he is as sick as a leper. So when he gets there, give him some hot soup and a big thumbs up, okay? All your Christian buddies back here say hello, especially those of us who are staying on as Caesar's guests in one of Rome's many fine prisons. I hope to be able to come see you soon.

Until then, take it easy. Never sleazy.
Paul

PAUL'S LETTER TO THE COLOSSIANS

 O MY HOLY BROTHERS in Colossae:

At a time when so many other churches are bringing shame to the game, I'm so grateful to hear about faithful Christians like you.

This is why (and I can't stress this enough) you have GOT to stick with Christianity. Despite what others may tell you, Christ is the only bridge between you and God. I'm warning you: you will run into eggheads who will use facts and clever arguments to get you to doubt your faith. Do not doubt your faith! Your soul will only make it into Heaven if it isn't tackled from behind by your brain.

And don't listen to those people in the church who still insist that you have to eat kosher foods, get circumcised, or go to the right festivals in order to become closer to God. Those are nothing but man-made rituals designed to show God how sorry we are for being human beings.

"Dragons are cool."

Jesus died on the cross so you could enter the Kingdom of God, so you don't need these rituals anymore. Jesus is your circumcision!

Don't expect puritanical rules to keep your actions holy, use your holiness to make your actions pure. Just as your heavenly souls were born with Christ's resurrection, so did your earthly bodies die at his crucifixion. Your sexual debauchery, your anger, your greed (which is really just another form of idolatry), all of it died on the cross with our Savior.

So all these rules and false distinctions are meaningless now. There's no such thing as Jews or Greeks, circumcised or uncircumcised, slave or free. We're all members of Christ's family. Treat each other like family. That is all.

Well, that's it for now. I'm writing from prison, so Tychicus and Onesimus will pay you a visit on my behalf. Oh, before I go, Epaphras says "hey!" So do Justus, Demas and Luke, the doctor. Okay, enough shout-outs. If you get a chance, pass this letter on to the church in Laodicea. Swap it for the letter I wrote them.

Slapped in chains so that Christ may reign,
Paul

"This town isn't evil enough for both of us."

PAUL'S 1ST LETTER TO THE THESSALONIANS

EAR THESSALONIANS,
First of all, I just wanted to thank you guys for being so awesome. When I first showed up in Thessalonica, you were a bunch of idol-worshiping dildos, but now look at you! You are the most faithful and trustworthy Christians out there.

I wish all Christians were like you guys. Remember when we first met? Many of you insulted me or tried to beat me up, but even then, I didn't try to candy-coat my teachings or tell you what you wanted to hear, so you know I was being honest with you. I love you enough to infuriate you.

By the way, I'm sorry I had to leave you all as abruptly as I did. I heard that the law came down pretty hard on you after I left. I hope you don't get the idea that I somehow left you holding the bag. I tried to come back as soon as I heard, but Satan suddenly made me too sick to travel. You know how he can be.

It always makes me nervous to leave new Christians on their own, because you never know what they're going to get up to when you aren't around. So imagine how happy I was to hear that you guys haven't been seduced by false

"Stay on your toes. You don't know when I'll be back."

prophets or scared away by the cops. I am so proud of you.

I'm sorry to hear that some members of your congregation have died since the last time I was there. Unfortunately, because of their deaths, some of you are now questioning whether I might have been wrong when I said that Christ would return during your lifetime. Now, this is going to take a little explaining. It may seem like I was wrong, but I wasn't, because your friends aren't really dead! When Jesus comes roaring back, which will be any day now, he will bring your dead church members back to life so they can take part in all the fun. So you see, I was right after all. Christ is coming back and coming back during your lifetime, though you might be dead when he gets here.

Until then, assuming you're still alive, remember to keep it in your pants. I know that's not easy when you look around and see all these oily, tanned Greeks walking around half-naked, but chastity really is for the best. Jesus will be coming back soon, and when we all fly up to meet him in the air, trust me, you'll want to have your pants on.

In closing, we don't know the day, exactly, when Christ will be coming back, so the only way to not be taken by surprise is to live every day like it's the big one.

Keep those purity rings polished.
Paul

"Who's playing that awful harmonica?"

PAUL'S 2ND LETTER TO THE THESSALONIANS

EAR THESSALONIANS, Once again, I just wanted to say that I think you guys are great. Your faith in God, even as you are being persecuted, is an inspiration to us all. And believe me, Christ is taking down the names of everyone who is giving you trouble, and when he comes back, they are in deep shit. In fact, everyone who doesn't believe in Christ will be in deep shit. They will all be banished from the presence of the Lord, where they will live in eternal darkness, and slowly be crushed to death for all eternity. So cheer up!

I'm glad to see that my last letter did the trick and that you are all back on board with the idea that Christ will be returning soon. That said, don't dance around anxiously thinking every day is the big one. I know I've been adamant about Christ's imminent return, but some of you are clearly overdoing it.

I've received reports of people refusing to go to work because, hey, what's the point if Christ is coming back any day now? Ludicrous. When I was living among you, did you see me loafing around, just waiting for Jesus to come sweep me out of my sandals? No, you did not. I've worked hard all day every day so that when he does come back, the world will be a little more ready for him.

Besides, a lot of things still need to go down before Christ comes back. There will be this big rebellion, the Anti-Christ will show up…You know what? If somebody refuses to work, just don't feed them. I've had it with loafers.

Anyway, I hope things settle down and you can all go back to living your lives without people trying to beat you or stab you in the throat all the time. May God be with you. Silas and Timothy say hello.

Peace.
Paul

PAUL'S 1ˢᵀ LETTER TO TIMOTHY

Dear **Tim,**
I was wondering if you wouldn't mind talking to the Church of Ephesus for me? They seem to have fallen off the wagon again. Especially Hymenaeus and Alexander. Those two are so full of shit, it's coming out their ears. I've just about written them off to Satan. Anyway, I'd appreciate it if you could do me a solid and get Ephesus back in line.

Here's what I want you to tell them:

Guys, I don't want you using the open prayer time to score cheap shots on each other or to make political statements. The last thing I want is for the prayers to end in fist-fights or to bring the law down on us for no good reason. So no more "God, please help Simon to stop stealing dinner rolls" prayers. If you're going to mention someone by name in your prayer, say something nice about them.

As for you ladies, I'd prefer it if you didn't say anything at all.

"Stop praying for stupid stuff."

"If you ask me, he wasn't the world's best lawyer."

After all, the last time we let a woman teach religion, it got us kicked out of the Garden of Eden. Am I right, guys? Also, there's no need for you to wear all those fancy clothes and jewelry to church. It's not a fashion show. Frankly, I'd rather you deck yourselves out in good deeds and modesty. Those accessories never go out of style! (You can use that line if you want to.) Anyway, ladies, don't come to church to show off, or talk, or do much of anything, for that matter.

Also, Tim, make sure the bishops and deacons are good, upstanding men who've belonged to the church for a long time. They shouldn't be in it for the money, have a temper or a taste for the wine. They should only have one wife (each) and their kids should be pleasant and well-behaved. If a bishop can't even keep his own house in order, then how's he supposed to keep a whole church in line? In fact, even the rank and file members of the church need to be serious, upstanding Christians. I don't want to hear about churchgoers making lewd gestures during services or telling dirty jokes in the foyer. Put an end to that ASAP.

Be sure to teach everyone the scriptures, both so they'll have a better appreciation of their religion and so they'll know what to say when non-believers heckle them.

And make sure they treat the widows in the church well, but only if they're real widows. You know, like over the age of, say... sixty. If they're young and foxy, don't worry about them so much. Take care of orphans, though, whatever their age. God likes orphans.

If a member of the church happens to be a slave, make sure they behave and are hard workers. Nobody likes a lazy slave, and I don't want their masters blaming their surliness on Christianity. Conversely, if a church member happens to be a slave owner, he should treat his slaves fairly so

they'll think kindly of his religion and perhaps even think of joining.

As a rule of thumb, I like to publicly humiliate sinners. It makes everyone else afraid to get up to anything. Feel free to develop your own management style, though.

Also, don't believe any accusations made against church leaders unless there are multiple witnesses. The last thing we need is a lot of turnover at the top.

Finally, make sure people don't get too materialistic. The love of money is the root of all evil. Money is meaningless in the grand scheme of things. We came into this world with nothing, and that's precisely how we'll leave it.

Anyway, that's my advice. You've got your work cut out for you, Tim. One of the reasons I'm writing all these things down is that I don't know how much longer I'll be around, so I want to give advice and pass on my wisdom while I still can.

Keepin' it real,
Paul

PAUL'S 2ND LETTER TO TIMOTHY

 EY **TIM,**

Still in jail waiting for my case to be heard by the Emperor Nero. To be honest, things aren't looking so hot for me. Let's just say that I've seen a lot of freaky shit go down, so I'm not terribly optimistic about being released for good behavior.

Don't worry about me, though. I'm not afraid to die. Those who die with Christ will live with him. And those who deny him will be denied by him. And, whatever happens to me, I take genuine comfort in the fact that I have friends like you. Your mother Eunice and Grandma Lois have always had unshakable faith in God, and I see the same strength in you. You never take a day off from being a good Christian, unlike some guys I know.

People accuse us of being lazy. When I'm out preaching, sometimes they'll shout, "Deadbeat!" or "Get a job!" But you know what? Telling people about the gospel isn't just a job, it's *every* job. You've got to be willing to take a brick to the head and die, like a soldier. You have to play by the rules, like an athlete. And you've got to work hard every day hoping that someday you'll see a crop, just like a farmer. Who else has a job like that? I'm not ashamed to be some crank street preacher locked up in prison. You shouldn't be either, because I've got to be honest, if you stick with this gig, this is probably where you'll end up.

The calling proved to be too much for Demas, I'm afraid. He got spooked and left the church. But as I near the end of my own rope, I can look back with pride and say that I remained true to the game. And if I can do it, so can you. Just stay focused on the work. Don't let yourself be distracted by Hymenaeus and Philetus and their idiotic theory that Christ has already returned to Earth and is hiding somewhere.

Ironically, one of the ways in which we know that Christ's return is near is because of such false prophets. In the last days, people will be greedy, conceited, self-absorbed hedonists. Smooth-talking con-men will worm their way into people's houses and prey on the gullible. So steer clear of guys like that.

Also, I hope Trophimus is feeling better. Give my love to Prisca and Aquila. Do NOT give my love to Alexander the copper-maker. He knows what he did.

Eubulus says, "What's up?" When you come to visit (you are coming to visit, right?), could you bring me my coat and some books?

I'm really going to miss you, Tim. You're like the son I never had, and I would really love to see you one last time before I die.

Please hurry.
Paul

PAUL'S LETTER TO TITUS

 EY TITUS,

In case you were wondering, the reason I'm sending you to Crete was to see if you could muster up some good, honest, and hopefully sober men to lead the church there. I understand this is no easy task, especially on Crete.

You can't trust those people half the time, and the other half of the time, they're asleep. Crete is full of liars, cheats, and gluttons. So don't be afraid to use a firm hand with them. As I tell everyone, make sure they quit with the circumcisions and all the old Jewish traditions. As I've already explained ad nauseum, we're a new religion now. If I remember correctly, you were pretty happy when I told you that you didn't have to get circumcised, so pass the favor along, will you?

Make sure they respect your authority. When they call you by name, make sure they're actually saying "Titus" and not "Tight-Ass." Those people will keep you on your toes, believe me.

See if you can convince the men to keep it in their pants for a change. And try to get the women to cut down on the wine and gossip. Be sure to set a good example for the young people. Don't tell them to behave in a way you aren't willing to behave yourself. Trust me, teenagers can smell a hypocrite a mile away.

I know I've been kind of having a bit of a go at the Cretans, but the truth is that before I found Jesus, I was even worse than they are. Remind them, as I remind myself, that Jesus didn't give his life because we're so great that we deserve it, but because we are so awful that we need it.

One more thing: try not to get caught up in stupid arguments about genealogy, the law, or minute points about church doctrine. Those conversations are exhausting and futile. If somebody turns out to be a contrarian or a troublemaker, give them a couple of warnings and then ban them from the church. Don't let a few itchy lice turn into a full-blown case of the crabs.

Everyone here is really pulling for you. I'll send someone soon to relieve you.

Holy hugs,
Paul

PAUL'S LETTER TO PHILEMON

 EAR PHILEMON,

How's everything going on your end? Good, I hope. Unfortunately, things aren't so great for me right now. You guessed it, I'm in jail! Although, I like to think of myself, not as being a prisoner of the Romans, but as a prisoner of Jesus Christ. After all, if Christ wanted me to be free, I'd be out, right? So, when you think about it that way, I guess I don't mind doing time if I can do it at the Jesus Christ Correctional Facility for Men.

Oh, guess who's been visiting me here in jail? Your old slave, Onesimus! In fact, I am kind of writing this letter on his behalf. Look, I know Onesimus ran away from you and that wasn't cool. But from the sound of it, you weren't all laughs and tickle-fights, either. At any rate, Onesimus has been a big help, so do right by him when he comes back, okay? DO NOT KILL HIM. (I'm totally reading your mind right now, aren't I?)

What's more, since he's a fellow Christian, you really ought to treat Onesimus more like a brother than a slave, anyway. Perhaps you should even consider freeing him. Or better yet, you could loan him to me. Like I said, he's been a big help.

In any case, go easy on him. If he owes you any money or has caused you any damage, charge it to me. True, you kind of already owe me one for that whole salvation/eternal life thing, but whatever, I'll still pay you if you really want me to.

Anyway, Luke and Mark say hello, as does Epaphras, who is also under Christ-arrest with me.

Stay golden,
Paul

PART EIGHT
OTHER ASSORTED LETTERS & VISIONS

In which the Romans get a little creative with the Christian problem, false prophets run amok, and the world comes to a fiery, insect-filled end.

F COURSE, PAUL WASN'T THE ONLY ONE WRITING ABOUT Christianity. He wasn't even the movement's leader. If that title belonged to anyone, it would've been James, who ran the church in Jerusalem and was the brother of Jesus Christ. And, as is clear from their letters, Paul and James didn't always agree. Paul thought Christianity had rendered all the old Jewish traditions obsolete, whereas James and many of the old disciples still considered themselves to be Jews first, and still beholden to Jewish laws and traditions.

Given the divisions in the church, most of these letters were written to warn Christians about false prophets, and to encourage them to stay strong as they faced persecution from the Roman Empire.

The Romans tried to be tolerant. They really wanted to be thought of as the cool empire, but there were two things they absolutely could not abide: revolts and people cheating on their taxes.

Many Christians refused to sacrifice to the Roman gods. To the Romans, who relied on the goodwill of Jupiter or Neptune or Artemis for good trade, weather, or harvests, sacrificing to these gods was tantamount to paying your taxes, and they couldn't figure out why the Christians were being such insufferable buttholes. Because of their refusal to sacrifice to the local gods, many Christians were convicted, ironically, of atheism. For their punishment, they were beaten, imprisoned or fed to wild animals during the matinee before the gladiator fights.

The Emperor Nero came to power in 54 CE, and he really ramped up the persecution, blaming the Christians for setting the Great Fire of Rome. In retaliation, he lit his parties with human torches, the burning bodies of hundreds of Christians.

To make matters worse, the Jews revolted against Roman rule in 66 CE, temporarily evicting the Romans from Jerusalem. At that point, the Romans were done putting up with these God-worshipers. After putting down the revolt, killing tens of thousands of Jews in the process, and basically outlawing the Jewish religion, they destroyed the Temple of Solomon. This was a shock, not only for Jews, but also for Christians, many of whom were basically Jews for Jesus. The Romans had destroyed God's home on Earth!

Meanwhile, a man named John had been living in a cave on the island of Patmos. When he heard that the Temple had been destroyed, that his Jewish countrymen were being slaughtered, and that his fellow Christians were being used as cat food, he thought that he was witnessing nothing less than the end of the world. That Jesus surely had to come back now, or there would be nothing left to come back to. So he wrote a book called "Revelation" describing his vision of the imminent end of the world.

THE LETTER TO THE HEBREWS

ERE'S THE NEWS, Jews: I wanted to take this opportunity to address some lingering questions regarding your conversion from Judaism to the Christian faith. The FAQ is below, please pass it around among yourselves.

Q: *You told us that Jesus was coming back any day, and that was, like, decades ago. What's the deal?*

A: What's the hurry? You got fish sticks in the oven? Don't worry, Jesus will come back when he's good and ready. In the meantime, do NOT flake out on the Son of God. Remember when your ancestors got sick of waiting for Moses to come down from Mount Sinai? They panicked and started making golden calves and idols, and look what happened to them. They spilled the hooch and screwed the pooch. The entire nation spent the next forty years lost in the desert. So don't make the same mistake twice.

Q: *Your teachings about the nature of Christ are often simplistic and, to be frank, vaguely insulting to our intelligence. We miss the richly complicated debates we used to have about the Torah.*

A: That's more of a comment than a question, actually. But to respond: of course our teachings are simplistic! You are babies in the Christian religion. As babies, you've got to

learn to drink milk before you can move on to solid food. Once you've mastered the basics of salvation and the forgiveness of sin, then we can get down to debating the finer points of Christian ethics and theology. Besides, if the old Jewish scriptures were doing such a great job of answering your questions, why did you turn to Christianity to begin with?

Q: *It's getting kind of dangerous to be a Christian. Remind us why we need Jesus again? Didn't God make all the same promises to us as Jews? Can't we just go back to being Jews if we want to?*

A: Do not let yourself be scared away from the Christian faith. Hearing the teachings of Christ, accepting them, and then changing your mind is like crucifying Jesus all over again. If there's one thing Christ hates, it's a tease.

Besides, being a Jew does not entitle you to the same promises as being a Christian. It's like the old Temple. Remember how everybody could come into the lower level of the Temple, but then there was the holy chamber in which only the priests could enter, and inside that was the Holy of Holies where God himself lived and where only the High Priest could go in? Heaven is like that.

Through simple acts of faith like sacrificing goats and sheep, we can all approach God in some basic, entry-level way. But dead goats only get you so far. After that, there's a higher level, a sort of Admiral's Lounge, reserved only for the top performers. Guys like Moses, Noah, and Abraham, people with such enormous faith that they were willing to do whatever weirdness God asked of them—like build a ship in the middle of nowhere, or kill their only son in a sacrifice. Stuff like that.

Finally, there's an inner sanctum, a Holy of Holies where God himself lives. And the only one who can go in there and be with God is Jesus Christ.

Because he is the Son of God, Jesus can approach God in a way we cannot. And that's why if we ever want to get into the Holy of Holies and be with God himself, we need to get on Jesus Christ's guest list. Following the old laws and customs just isn't going to cut it. Not if you want the full Heaven experience.

Okay, I hope this FAQ clears everything up. If there's anything else you're confused about, please take it up with your bishop or deacon.

THE LETTER OF JAMES

To: Christians everywhere

From: James
         Brother of Jesus Christ
         Leader of the Church

Re: Some damn good advice

'VE HEARD THAT a lot of you have been arrested, beaten up, and imprisoned simply for being Christians. Do you know what I say to that? Good! If you want sympathy, you can find it in the dictionary between shit and syphilis. God wants true believers. Hardship and persecution are the only things that keep the dabblers and dilettantes away. If you're willing to be burned at the stake or eaten alive by baboons for your faith, then you're obviously not in it for the free donuts and communion wine.

Maybe that's why Christianity isn't such a hot religion for rich people. They have so much to lose, and to serve Christ, you have to be willing to lose it all. Keep that in mind the next time a rich man wants special treatment. If anyone's going to sell you out to the cops, it'll be the rich guy who bought the front pew, not the guy in the greasy loincloth you made sit in the back. Besides, if the loincloth guy is good enough to sit by God's side in Heaven, then who are you to tell him to move to the back of the church?

Also, despite whatever Paul may have told you, don't think that having faith in Jesus Christ means you can simply stumble into Heaven like a drunk crashing on the couch. God doesn't give out medals just for believing the right things. You think believing in God makes you hot gravy? It doesn't. Even the *devil* believes in God. So the Almighty isn't terribly blown away by your willingness to acknowledge his existence.

What God wants from you isn't your belief, but your dedication. Faith is nice, but by itself, it's worthless. If you're one of these Christians who's full of faith, but who lets widows and orphans starve to death, you need to either start doing Christ's work or start calling yourself something else. Faith without action is dead.

There is no proof of your faith *except* for action.

And don't try to impress us with big talk about all the wonderful things you're going to do in the future. The future is a bank without any deposits. Life is what you're doing *now*, not what you plan to do later. Don't try to excuse yourself from the hard work of feeding and clothing people today because you'll make up for it tomorrow. Hell, you don't even know if you'll be alive tomorrow. A Christian who hears the teachings of Christ and doesn't act on them is like a guy who looks into a mirror but then forgets what he looks like the second he walks away.

Also, don't praise God with the same mouth you use to curse people. You can't be a good Christian and a hateful prick any more than you can be a tree which grows both figs and oranges. It's one fruit or the other, folks.

Remember, you're all brothers and sisters. You should be quick to listen, reluctant to speak, and slow as ketchup to get angry. Just as a forest fire can start with one tiny spark, a church can be destroyed by a few angry words. The road to Hell is paved with snappy comebacks, but as far as I know,

God never struck anyone down for being a good listener.

Nor should you judge each other. There is only one qualified judge in the entire Universe and that is God. So when you judge somebody, you're basically telling God that you can do his job better.

Finally, don't waste your life chasing money. It just makes you fat and untrustworthy. I would like to remind you that we are living in the last days. So hoarding money at this point is sort of like scooping up poker chips aboard a sinking ship.

Hey, I'm sorry if I seemed a little glib earlier about the hardships and persecutions you are facing. I know you're suffering. My point is that as hard as life is for you right now, it will all be worth it in the end. Just stay the course a little longer for soon we will all be safe together in the Kingdom of God. Christ will lead his ants to the picnic, I promise.

THE 1ˢᵀ EPISTLE OF PETER

O ALL MY FRIENDS IN ASIA:

One of you brought up an interesting question the other day: if faith in Jesus Christ is the only way to get into Heaven, then what about all the people who died before Christ was born? Do they go to Hell? I think I might have an answer for that:

After Jesus was crucified, it was a good three days before he came back from the dead. If I know Jesus, he probably spent those three days in the netherworld, preaching to all the dead souls so they could believe in him, too. It makes sense and it's totally like something he would do. So I wouldn't worry about the dead too much. They're probably already partying up in Heaven.

I've heard the stories about how you are being fed to lions in the arena. This is, hands down,

"Do you need anything?"

the worst time to be a Christian. Though, admittedly, it is a pretty magical time to be a lion. I know what you're going through, and I've heard you beg for salvation and cry out for Christ's mercy. Over the years, I've come to know and love you all. And that's why it kills me to say what I have to tell you now: Christ is not going to save you.

When somebody is asked to die for a god they don't truly believe in, they drop him faster than a snake with herpes. Only people who worship the living Son of God are willing to give their very lives for him. I'm sorry, but when all is said and done, it won't be your preaching, or your morality that brings people to Christ. It will be your *death*. Like Christ before you, you must suffer so your tormentors can see the Kingdom of God.

I know this sounds nuts, especially considering what the law is doing to you, but it is essential that you be good, law-abiding citizens. I don't care how sadistic the government is, or how ruthless your slave owner or husband may be. You have to put up with it so that when you are finally led away to die for Christ, people will know that you are innocent of all else, and that it is for your faith alone that you die.

It's a lot to ask of you, and it breaks my heart to ask it. But don't be afraid of the trials which await you. Everyone suffers. The only difference is that evil men suffer from their punishment, while good men suffer from their persecution.

The final judgment is very near. I can hear the fire roaring. You must keep each other strong as you face the end together. Satan lurks behind you like a lion (sorry, poorly chosen analogy, I know), probing, pawing, trying to single out the weak before going in for the kill. You must stand together like a mighty herd, or he will pick you off, one by one.

I wish I had happier news. I love you all.

Until we meet again in this life or the next,
Peter

THE 2ND EPISTLE OF PETER

TO MY FRIENDS IN THE seven churches of Asia: In my last letter, I got a little carried away and implied that the world was about to come to an end. I'm sorry if I misled you. Hopefully none of you made any major purchases.

Some of you may now feel a little silly for telling your friends and coworkers about the imminent end of the world. But you know what? Don't worry about what non-believers think about you. People will always mock your faith. They'll say things like, "Hey, Elijah, who's going to win the chariot race?" or, "Hey, is the world going to end today, or is it okay for me for me to plant artichokes?"

Don't let them get to you. Nobody knows the exact day or hour, Jesus will come back and he does, he will come like a thief in the night. Or maybe a ninja. At any rate, nobody will see it coming. Not knowing when Jesus is coming back does not mean you get to relax and get sloppy. In fact, it means the opposite: you need to live as if he could show up at any moment.

"Did I say the end of the world was this Saturday? I meant to say next Saturday."

So remain vigilant. Especially now that the church seems to have become rotten with false prophets, eager to prey upon your disappointment. The sad thing is that a lot of these false prophets used to be good, upstanding Christians. But I guess they just couldn't help but go back to their old sinful ways. They are like dogs returning to their vomit. A pig returning to her shit. Sorry, I'm getting carried away again.

Don't get too chummy with these people. If God turned Sodom & Gomorrah into charcoal because of a few smooth boys, then imagine what he has in store for false prophets. You've all come so far, I'd hate to see someone trip you up this close to the finish line.

I love you, Asians! You are all my pitted cherries.

Peter

THE 1ˢᵀ LETTER OF JOHN

 I ALL,

Okay, there seems to be a lot of confusion about just who Jesus was, or what he came to Earth to do, so let me set the record straight:

Jesus was an actual man. Flesh and blood. He wasn't an angel, or some spirit dude, as has been suggested in some circles. Frankly, some of you have been getting a little too new-agey for my liking. If somebody tells you that Jesus

was a ghost, a mermaid, or that he lives inside a pinecone, or anything weird like that, there are some easy ways to tell if this person is on the level.

First and foremost, a real disciple of Christ will embody the teachings of Christ. If someone preaches the Resurrected Christ during the day and hits the whorehouse at night, they have no credibility. A lot of fun, but no credibility. Also, don't believe anybody who says that you don't have to follow Christ in order to get into Heaven. That's pure donkey balls. And, whatever you do, don't believe anyone who says Jesus wasn't a real flesh and blood man! I don't know why, but this really boils me up.

In the end, the best way to tell if someone was truly sent by Christ is if they love people. Loving people was like Christ's number one thing. So if someone acts hatefully towards people, then he clearly has no idea what Christ was all about.

John

"Our religion is about love, you moron."

THE 2ND LETTER OF JOHN

 o **GOD'S SPECIAL** Lady (You Know Who You Are!):

Okay, I know you're a church and not a woman, but I've already made the metaphor so now I'm going to run with it. Woman, I'm so glad to see that your children are growing up true and strong. They're really great kids, obeying God's commandments and all that. Nice! Quite a loving brood, too. And the most important of Christ's teachings, of course, is that we love one another.

As I mentioned in my last letter, there are a lot of false prophets out there. Gnostics, hippies, and God-knows-what-else. You're such a great lady, I'd hate to see your faith derailed by one of these heretics. If somebody tells you that you don't need Christ to get into Heaven, don't believe them. They are a false prophet. And if someone claims that Christ wasn't a real human being, but some sort of spirit/ghost, then he's probably a false prophet, too. Who knows? Maybe even the Antichrist. In any case, don't let him in the house.

I have so much more to say to you, but I'm running low on paper and ink, so the rest will have to wait until I see you face to face, which I hope will be soon.

Love,
John

"I wish I were writing to a woman… that'd be nice."

THE 3RD LETTER OF JOHN

DEAR **G**AIUS,

I hope this letter finds you well. I just wanted to say that I'm really impressed by how you've been welcoming traveling Christians into your home, some of whom don't even speak your language. They may not understand your words, but nothing says "Welcome!" quite like a hot meal and a good foot scrub.

It's always good when Christians can put aside their differences to help each other. The less we have to rely on pagans for help, the better. When a non-believer takes you in, they may start out feeding you dinner or making your bed, but it's just a matter of time before they want you to join in their blood dances, or chicken worship, or whatever. Besides, what does it say about us when heathens are nicer to Christians than we are?

Speaking of which, what's the deal with Diotrephes? Why is he being such a dick? He won't even let me come speak at his church. Is he afraid I'll upstage him? I'll bet that's it, isn't it? He's a total hater. He's all holier-than-thou in church but then he doesn't let traveling Christians stay in his house. What's more, he doesn't even let his parishioners take them in. I mean, not lending a hand is one thing, but how much of a prick do you have to be to keep others from helping out?

Anyway, I've got a lot more to say, but as usual, I don't have much paper and ink to spare, so I'd better keep it short. Hopefully, I'll see you soon.

Friends in Faith Forever,
John

"Could somebody out there bring me some paper?"

THE EPISTLE OF JUDE

To: All Bishops and Regional Managers, Church of Jesus Christ, Eastern Mediterranean Division
From: Jude, Brother of James
Re: Quality Control

Gentlemen:

IRST OF ALL, LET ME congratulate you all on another successful year. The Church continues to grow, due in no small part to your dedication. However, I would like to take this opportunity to caution you against cutting corners simply for the sake of posting higher membership numbers.

It has come to my attention that some of your churches are practically filled to the rafters with perverts and troublemakers. These people will only give you a bad reputation, lead your parishioners astray, and ruin your love feasts.

I've heard about some people joining the church so they can stop in for a quick absolution after a long day of idolatry and fornication. Others seem to think that the church is some sort of creative writing workshop where they can come up with whatever crazy doctrine they want to and have it treated like holy scripture.

These false prophets are just more proof that the end of the world is at hand.

Do not tolerate such people. Just because they're Christians doesn't mean God likes them. Remember, God rescued the Jews from Egypt only to knock a few of them off later, and if God doesn't want someone around, you shouldn't either.

This is not to say that you shouldn't try to bring new members into the fold. Growth is good. Getting asses in the seats is what the church is all about. But let the message be what draws the people in. Don't lose the coop to catch a chicken.

In closing, I'd like to thank you all for your continued hard work. Here's to another great year.

P.S. While I've got you, I've been working on a new song. I've only written a few verses, but I think it's really good! It starts out like this:
Majesty and power,
Through Jesus Christ!
Staying pure forever…

That's all I've got so far. When I'm finished, I'll send it off so you can sing it in church.

THE BOOK OF REVELATION

O THE SEVEN CHURCHES of Asia:

The good news is that your persecution won't last much longer. The bad news is that's because you'll all be dead soon. That's right, the end of the world we've all been waiting for is finally here! I was sitting here in my cave, minding my own business, serving time under cave-arrest, when an angel of the Lord appeared and gave me the following revelation:

There's this giant book in Heaven with seven chapters and each chapter is sealed shut. When the seals are broken and the book is opened, all hell will break loose. The first four seals will release the Four Horsemen of the Apocalypse: Conquest, War, Famine, and Death. That last horseman, Death, is a real son of a bitch, so steer clear of him if you can. By the time he's done, one-quarter of the human race will be dead. Cities will be destroyed. Practically everyone will be living outside and digging through trash. Dogs will be largely unaffected by the Apocalypse.

Then Christ will open the rest of the seals, none of which are very nice. When the fifth seal is cracked, all the Christians who were killed for their faith will come back to life. They'll barely have their faces back before they start begging God to avenge their deaths. God will cave in to the peer pressure, and when the sixth seal is opened, he will unleash horrible earthquakes, blacken the sun, and turn the moon blood red. Millions of people will die. Things will get so rough that people will hide in caves and beg the mountains to fall on them.

Finally, when the seventh seal is opened, the world will get a breather from all the wars, earthquakes and death. This period of peace will last for a whole thirty minutes. Once break-time is over, seven angels will start blowing their trumpets, and then it's right back to falling stars, hailstones made of blood, and monsters ripping the heads off babies.

While this is happening, a pregnant woman will give birth to a son. But this is no place to have a baby.

A red dragon with seven heads will be watching, waiting for his chance to eat the boy when he pops out.

But the pregnant lady will snatch the baby out of the dragon's jaws and escape up to Heaven. The dragon will chase them into Heaven, but God will be all like, "What's that dragon doing up here?" The angels will swat at it with brooms, shooing it away. Once they throw the dragon back to the ground, it'll skulk around, vowing to get revenge on all the woman's children who are still down on Earth.

(Psst. Just in case you're wondering if I've been huffing frankincense, I am actually writing in code. The dragon, *as I'm sure you've figured out by now, is Satan. The woman is Israel, and her son is our Messiah, Jesus Christ. Don't tell anyone!)*

To make life miserable for the woman's children, the dragon will raise two beasts. The first beast will have seven heads and ten horns, and he'll have obscenities scrawled on each of his heads. He will rule the world. Needless to say, a state ruled by an obscenity-laden seven-headed beast won't be a model of sensible, moderate governance.

(Psst. I'm writing in code again! The first beast is an allegory for the Roman Empire. Jesus Christ escaped from Satan, so now Satan is using the Romans to wage war on Israel's children.

"Encore! Encore!"

They destroyed the Temple, and because we won't worship the Emperor as a god, Nero is killing Christians like he's trying to win a prize at the county fair. Again, don't tell the Romans I said ANY OF THIS. I'm already under cave-arrest. I don't need any more trouble.)

Then the dragon will send a second beast. This beast has the horns of a lamb and goes by the number 666. *(For those of you who didn't go to Hebrew school, that is the alphanumeric equivalent of the Emperor Nero's name.)* This beast is a false prophet. He will try to force everyone to worship the first beast as a god. But don't do it, or God...well, let's just say things will get very weird for you.

The Roman Emp—uh, I mean the Beast and his false prophet and all the kings of the world will meet on a battlefield known as Armageddon to destroy God's people, once and for all. And that is when Jesus Christ will finally come back to Earth. He'll come riding out of Heaven on a white horse with a sword in his hand, Lord-of-the-Rings style. He'll kill every single soldier in the Roman army and use their weapons for firewood. Then he will dropkick the Beast and his false prophet straight into the Lake of Fire. I

know this doesn't sound very much like the Jesus you know and love, but hey, the guy's sick of being pushed around.

And that's it, the world will be pretty much finished.

So what was it all about then? Why did God even bother creating plants and animals and Greeks? Why waste the time leading Moses and his nation of hikers out of Egypt? All those years of wandering through the desert to come to Israel, to set up a kingdom under David and Solomon? What was the point of suffering under the Babylonians for forty years and coming back and rebuilding the Temple? Why did God send Elijah and Daniel and John the Baptist and finally, his son, Jesus Christ? Was it all just so he could kill the human race off with earthquakes and falling stars and skin diseases?

No, it wasn't. God did not create people just to exterminate them. Believe it or not, it's not out of anger that God will destroy the world, but love.

When the world you've known and hated has finally been destroyed, God can finally come back to Earth and start over with a clean slate. God will bring all the dead Christians back to life and give the martyrs sweet government jobs. Then he will rule the entire world as the Kingdom of God, and take care of us like hamsters, like he did in the beginning.

The world will be just like it was at the Garden of Eden. Only a little more crowded this time…and with fewer talking snakes.

AFTERWORD

NE AFTERNOON I WAS HAVING DRINKS WITH SHANNON Wheeler (yes, we're afternoon drinkers). I'm not sure how it came up, but I mentioned that I had summarized the Book of Job in three paragraphs for a friend who had never heard the story. Unexpectedly, Shannon said, "You should do that to the entire Bible. I'll draw cartoons for it." And that is how this book was born. I figured it would be easy. I'd grown up reading the Bible, and how long could it possibly take to write three paragraphs per book? That was three years ago.

It wasn't long before I realized that I could recreate the Bible from memory about as well as my ass can chew gum. What's more, three paragraphs wasn't enough to do justice to any but a handful of the Bible's sixty-six books. Thus began two years of study, reading the entire Bible from front to back twice, constant editing and revision, and hassling PHD candidates for free advice. This had become a quest to not make this just a collection of Bible stories, but to really understand the book on a meaningful level. To give some insight into this ubiquitous, but somehow unknown, holy book.

Some of the Bible translated easily into this truncated, hyper-condensed medium. Books like Ruth, Job, and Esther had a nice central narrative with a tidy ending and were easy to squeeze into Biblical concentrate. Other books didn't have much of a plot, but an embarrassing depth of good material to work with. Proverbs, Ecclesiastes, and James were easy to write simply because the originals were so witty and profound.

Other books stubbornly resisted this process. How does one condense a book like Psalms, which is just a collection of songs? This one had me baffled until it occurred to me to present it as you would any collection of 150 classic songs: as a greatest hits boxset. The most difficult book to write, though, was the Book of Revelation. A lot of it reads like a really bad game of *Dungeons & Dragons*. It was by far the hardest book for me to get a handle on. It was so cryptic, confusing, and open to interpretation—how could I hope to get it right? Luckily, at this point I encountered Elaine Pagels' utterly invaluable *Revelations: Visions, Prophecy, and Politics in the Book of Revelation*. For the first time in my life, I felt I understood this book, not as predictions of events thousands of years in the future, but rather, as the prayer of a man who had witnessed the destruction of everything he loved and thought the end of the world was at hand. To me, this made the book infinitely more powerful, more human, than anything televangelists or the *Left Behind* series had to offer.

I wasn't sure how this book would be received. It's highly irreverent, for one thing. If I had a religion, I suppose I would call it Irreverence. I feel that the sacred exists only at the expense of the truth. So I always feel it my personal mission to try to catch things just as they're getting out of bed, to get a look at the truth before it puts its makeup on. What I really wanted to accomplish with this book was to not only to make the Bible easy to understand, but to throw out all its sacred baggage so we could really get to know it. To not mince words about God's anger management problems, or his weird pseudo-marriage with the Jews. To be perfectly frank in reflecting Paul's hilarious sexism, or how douchey and self-serving King David could be. I realized that some people would not take this well.

Mostly to promote the book, but in part to gauge the reaction, Shannon and I made some samplers containing early versions of a few of the selections from this book. And they did make some people angry. But I was surprised to discover that far more of the people we gave them out to really liked them. As it turns out, most Christians actually have a pretty good sense of humor about the Bible. One pastor snapped up about a dozen samplers to give to members of his congregation, and a sixty-nine year-old nun told me that she was going use the sampler in teaching her Bible class. They seemed to get that that the book's blunt, and often profane, sense of humor was an attempt at honesty rather than assassination.

One of these samplers happened to fall into the hands of Chris Staros at Top Shelf Productions, who wrote Shannon and I a really nice e-mail expressing interest in publishing the book. Once we agreed to publish the book with Top Shelf, the first question to come up was "What do we call it?" After a few abortive suggestions, all of which I'm glad we turned down, we all started to focus in on "God Is Disappointed in You," which is the perfect title for this book, because if I had to condense the entire Bible down to a single phrase, that would be it.

This journey has taken three years of research and writing, of second-guessing whether words like "shit" and "tip-slip" belong in the Bible, of befuddlement and epiphany. I don't claim that this book was the beneficiary of divine intervention, though there were moments when it sure felt like it. Or maybe "divine intervention" is simply what we call our hard work, hand-wringing, and the hope that we somehow got it right.

—Mark Russell

Mark Russell lives in Portland, Oregon, where he writes and occasionally draws cartoons. His work has previously appeared in *McSweeney's*, *Bear Deluxe*, *Unshod Quills*, *Blog of the Damned*, and several now-defunct magazines.

Follow Mark Russell on Twitter: @Manruss.

Shannon Wheeler is the creator of the comic book and opera *Too Much Coffee Man*. A variety of publications have run his weekly comic and single panel gag cartoons including *The New Yorker* and *The Onion*. Wheeler currently lives in Portland, Oregon, with his cats, chickens, bees, girlfriend, and children. He has multiple books that are easy to find.

Follow Shannon Wheeler on Twitter: @MuchCoffee. His website is www.TMCM.com.